SPECIAL EDITION FOR

YOUNG READERS

The Golden Book of   *America*

Collection of E. J. Rousuck; Courtesy Book-of-the-Month Club

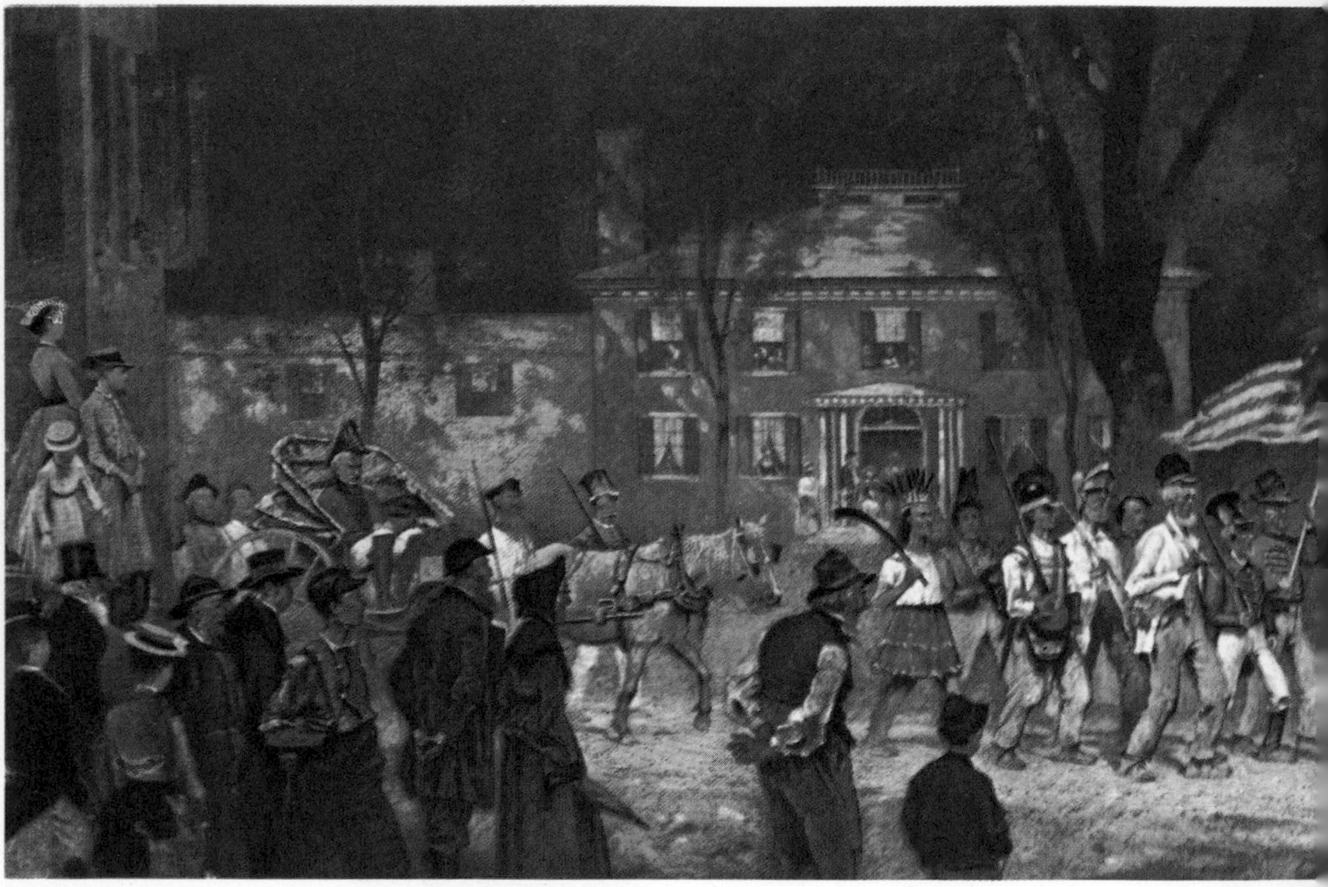

The Golden Book of

AMERICA

Stories from Our Country's Past

Adapted for Young Readers by IRWIN SHAPIRO

from the pages of AMERICAN HERITAGE

THE MAGAZINE OF HISTORY

With a Foreword by BRUCE CATTON

SIMON AND SCHUSTER · NEW YORK

ACKNOWLEDGMENTS

DID COLUMBUS DISCOVER AMERICA? From *Was America Discovered Before Columbus?* by Alvin M. Josephy, Jr. (April, 1955: Vol. VI, No. 3).

THE SECRET LIFE OF THE AMERICAN INDIAN. From *Myths That Hide the American Indian* by Oliver La Farge (October, 1956: Vol. VII, No. 6) and *People of the Long House* by Paul A. W. Wallace (February, 1955: Vol. VI, No. 2).

LA SALLE, THE LAKES, AND THE MISSISSIPPI. From *La Salle on the Mississippi: A Portfolio of Paintings by George Catlin* and *La Salle and the Discovery of the Great West* (April, 1957: Vol. VIII, No. 3), from Francis Parkman's *The Discovery of the Great West.*

HIGHWAYMEN OF THE SEAS. From *War Makes Thieves, Peace Hangs Them* by Roger Burlingame (February, 1957: Vol. VIII, No. 2).

THE NEW WORLD CHANGES WARFARE. From *The End of Formalized Warfare* by Louis Morton (August, 1955: Vol. VI, No. 5).

THE YANKEES TAKE LOUISBOURG. From *Yankee Gunners at Louisbourg* by Fairfax Downey (February, 1955: Vol. VI, No. 2).

DANIEL BOONE, HERO. From *Ghost Writer to Daniel Boone* by John Walton (October, 1955: Vol. VI, No. 6).

ELI WHITNEY'S MAGIC MACHINES. From *Eli Whitney: Nemesis of the South* by Arnold Whitridge (April, 1955: Vol. VI, No. 3).

WASHINGTON'S SPY AT TRENTON. From *A Spy for Washington* by Leonard Falkner (August, 1957: Vol. VIII, No. 5).

THE PATRIOT PAINTER. From *The Peales* by Oliver Jensen (April, 1955: Vol. VI, No. 3).

THE GREAT SEA WAR. From an article of the same name by Robert M. Lunny (April, 1956: Vol. VII, No. 3).

OLD HICKORY AT NEW ORLEANS. From *Victory at New Orleans* by C. S. Forester (August, 1957: Vol. VIII, No. 5).

MADE FOR AMERICA. From an article of the same name by Ruth B. Davidson (August, 1955: Vol. VI, No. 5).

SALEM'S SHIPS SAILED EAST. From *To the Farthest Port of the Rich East* by Charles H. P. Copeland (February, 1955: Vol. VI, No. 2).

PAINTERS OF THE WEST. From *Painters of the Plains* by Eugene Kingman (December, 1954: Vol. VI, No. 1).

HOW THEY KILLED THE BUFFALO. From an article of the same name by Wayne Gard (August, 1956: Vol. VII, No. 5).

THE MOUNTAIN MEN. From *The Wild Freedom of the Mountain Men* by William Brandon (August, 1955: Vol. VI, No. 5).

PATHFINDER OF THE WEST. From *A Record Filled with Sunlight* by Allan Nevins (June, 1956: Vol. VII, No. 4).

A NOSEGAY OF VALENTINES. From an article of the same name (February, 1955: Vol. VI, No. 2).

BUILT FOR SPEED. From *The Drive for Speed at Sea* by Alan Villiers (October, 1955: Vol. VI, No. 6).

THE FIRST DUDE RANCH TRIP. From *First "Dude Ranch" Trip to the Untamed West* by Alvin M. Josephy, Jr. (February, 1956: Vol. VII, No. 2).

THE HARD-LUCK FRIGATE. From an article of the same name by A. B. C. Whipple (February, 1956: Vol. VII, No. 2).

IT WAS FUN TO BE A SOLDIER. From an article of the same name by Martha Swain (August, 1956: Vol. VII, No. 5).

GENERALS OF THE UNION. From *This Hallowed Ground* by Bruce Catton (October, 1956: Vol. VII, No. 6).

GENERALS OF THE CONFEDERACY. From *Mary Custis Lee's Arlington* by Elizabeth Dabney Coleman (Spring, 1954: Vol. V, No. 3).

THE BATTLE OF THE IRONCLADS. From *I Fired the First Gun and Thus Commenced the Great Battle* by Lieutenant S. Dana Greene. Reprinted through the courtesy of Warren C. Shearman (June, 1957: Vol. VIII, No. 4).

GENERAL LEE'S TWO WARS. From *General Lee's Unsolved Problem* by Clifford Dowdey (April, 1955: Vol. VI, No. 3).

DEATH ON THE DARK RIVER. From an article of the same name by Cedric A. Larson (October, 1955: Vol. VI, No. 6).

IT HAPPENS EVERY FOUR YEARS. From an article of the same name by Roy F. Nichols (June, 1956: Vol. VII, No. 4).

THE OVERLAND STAGE. From *Great Days of the Overland Stage* by W. Eugene Hollon (June, 1957: Vol. VIII, No. 4).

THE MAN WHO KILLED CUSTER. From an article of the same name by Stanley Vestal (February, 1957: Vol. VIII, No. 2).

THE OLD COUNTRY STORE. From *Holiday Time at the Old Country Store* (December, 1954: Vol. VI, No. 1) and *Who Put the Borax in Dr. Wiley's Butter?* by Gerald H. Carson (August, 1956: Vol. VII, No. 5).

THE CAMERA LOOKS AT AMERICA. From *The Camera Opens Its Eye on America* by D. Jay Culver (December, 1956: Vol. VIII, No. 1).

BUILDERS FOR THE CARRIAGE TRADE. From an article of the same name by Paul H. Downing and Harrison Kinney (October, 1956: Vol. VII, No. 6).

THE OLD FALL RIVER LINE. From an article of the same name by Oliver Jensen (December, 1954: Vol. VI, No. 1).

WHEN THE OLD STREETS TALKED. From an article of the same name (June, 1955: Vol. VI, No. 4).

THE PROUD, FIGHTING FIREMEN. From *How Steam Blew the Rowdies out of the Fire Department* by Robert S. Holzman (December, 1955: Vol. VII, No. 1).

THE GREAT BICYCLE CRAZE. From an article of the same name by Fred C. Kelly (December, 1956: Vol. VIII, No. 1).

AMERICAN POSTERS. From *Posters: U.S.A.* (December, 1955: Vol. VII, No. 1).

ADVENTURE FOR A NICKEL. From *Dime Novels* by Mary Noel (February, 1956: Vol. VII, No. 2).

BUILDING THE BIG BRIDGE. From *When They Built the Big Bridge* by Frances Williams Browin (October, 1956: Vol. VII, No. 6).

HERE COMES THE TRAIN! From *Farewell to Steam* by Oliver Jensen (December, 1957: Vol. IX, No. 1).

THE BIRDMEN AT BELMONT. From *The Birdmen at Belmont Park* by Thomas Naughton (April, 1956: Vol. VII, No. 3).

A LINER, A U-BOAT, AND HISTORY. From *Chance or Destiny*, copyright, 1955, by Oscar Handlin (*American Heritage*, June, 1955: Vol. VI, No. 4).

LIGHT FOR LINCOLN'S STATUE. From an article of the same name by M. F. Cresson (February, 1956: Vol. VII, No. 2).

THE COVER DESIGN WAS ADAPTED FROM A HAND-PRINTED UNGLAZED CHINTZ BY GREEFF FABRICS, INC.

FIRST PRINTING

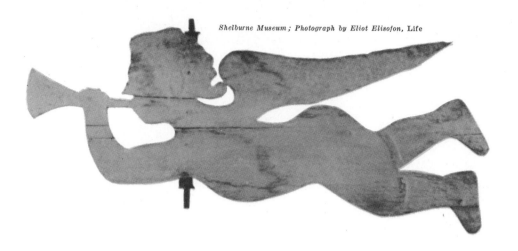

Foreword

Everything that we do in America is built on the lives of people we ourselves never saw. Our homes, food, clothing, schools, jobs—the games we play and the songs we sing, the very ideas we have about ourselves and the world we live in—all these have grown out of the things millions of Americans did in a time before our own. When we try to find out how those people lived, we are really trying to find out what we ourselves are all about.

So it is important to learn what those earlier Americans did. It can also be fun, because they did some interesting and exciting things. Taken altogether, their stories make up the record of a great country and a great people. Yet the separate items are very different, for the American record has everything in it—comedy and tragedy, greatness and folly, the profound and the simple, stories of high achievement and the accounts of ordinary people who were only trying to make a living and get a little enjoyment out of life. The individual stories fit together like the pieces of a jigsaw puzzle; but each separate piece is interesting on its own account.

The *American Heritage* magazine was founded on the idea that to record the great history of America one need not be solemn or dull; on the belief that the infinite assortment of incidents from the American past is entertaining as well as instructive; on the conviction that the glowing and revealing truth about America forms a mosaic of never-ending complexity and absorbing variety. Its editors have felt that each piece out of the golden mosaic has its own attractiveness and its own meaning, and that the continuity which binds them together is something that comes out of the American spirit itself.

The stories which appear in this collection have been carefully adapted to bring the past alive. They were chosen almost at random, the only connecting thread being the fact that each has to do with a part of the history of the American people.

There are stories about Indians, for example, and about early explorers, and about battles fought by American soldiers. There are stories about hunters and trappers and fur traders, about sailing ships and old-time steamboats, about the carriages people rode in, before the automobile was dreamed of. There are accounts of the gaudy Valentines that were once popular, about the dime novels that preceded today's comic books (and which, incidentally, were just about as bloodcurdling as any of the modern creations), and about the country store and its cracker-barrel debating societies which flourished in the era of isolated villages and unimproved dirt roads. There are, to illustrate these, more than 300 pictures, some of them serious and some of them emphatically otherwise. The aim has been to present samples of what American life was like in the days before we ourselves were here, so that we can understand how our country took its shape and direction and what it cost, in human terms, to put it all together.

The understanding is important, of course. Even more important, we believe, is the fact that each of these stories makes interesting reading in its own right. We don't, for instance, read about the romantic "mountain men" of the Old West just to improve our minds; we do it because they were bold, colorful men who risked their lives to earn a living at a time when half the continent was empty, unmapped, and dangerous. We read about the pirates who used to prowl the Atlantic coast not just because piracy was an important feature in early Colonial life, conditioned by the economic and social forces of the time; we read such stories because pirates, sinful though they were, make fascinating reading matter.

Taken altogether, however, these tales do make up a coherent story about American life. For an odd thing develops, in this examination of the American record: the whole of it is somehow greater than the sum of its parts. Each event stands by itself, yet each adds to the effect of the events which came before, slipping into place like the carefully carved block in the facade of a mighty building, each one touched by the eternally alive, constantly changing yet consistent vitality of the American spirit. The record is darkened by clouds and lit by sunlight, touched with tears and laughter by turn—a golden, imperishable record of a people moving on to make a great destiny out of the infinite variety of human dreams.

— BRUCE CATTON

Photograph by Eliot Elisofon, Life

Contents

Photograph by Eliot Elisofon, Life

Did Columbus Discover America? . . . 8

The Secret Life of the American
    Indian 12

La Salle, the Lakes, and the Mississippi 24

Highwaymen of the Seas 34

The New World Changes Warfare . . 40

The Yankees Take Louisbourg . . . 45

Daniel Boone, Hero 49

Eli Whitney's Magic Machines . . . 50

Washington's Spy at Trenton . . . 54

The Patriot Painter 58

The Great Sea War 62

Old Hickory at New Orleans 72

Made for America 76

Salem's Ships Sailed East 80

Painters of the West 85

How They Killed the Buffalo . . . 96

The Mountain Men 98

Pathfinder of the West 102

A Nosegay of Valentines 106

Built for Speed 112

The First Dude Ranch Trip 118

The Hard-Luck Frigate 120

It was Fun To Be a Soldier 122

Generals of the Union 132

Generals of the Confederacy 134

The Battle of the Ironclads 136

General Lee's Two Wars 140

Death on the Dark River 142

It Happens Every Four Years 144

The Overland Stage 152

The Man Who Killed Custer 154

The Old Country Store 156

The Camera Looks at America . . . 161

Builders for the Carriage Trade . . . 169

The Old Fall River Line 173

When the Old Streets Talked 178

The Proud, Fighting Firemen . . . 182

The Great Bicycle Craze 185

American Posters 187

Adventure for a Nickel 195

Building the Big Bridge 198

Here Comes the Train! 201

The Birdmen at Belmont 208

A Liner, a U-Boat, and History . . . 210

Light for Lincoln's Statue 212

INDEX 214

Did Columbus Discover America?

When Christopher Columbus set sail on his first voyage across the great Ocean Sea, one of his shipmates was Juan de la Cosa, owner of the *Santa Maria*. La Cosa must have heard the cry of "Tierra! Tierra!"— Land! Land!—that rang out in the early hours of October 12, 1492. And as dawn broke, he must have caught his first glimpse of the New World—the gleaming white beach of a little island in the Bahamas.

A year later, La Cosa again sailed to the New World with Columbus. On this voyage he was master chart maker and navigator of the *Niña*. By 1500 he was back in Europe, at the port of Santa Maria. There he made a map, trying for the first time to show the entire New World.

At the right of the map, which was painted on an ox hide, he carefully drew the coast of Europe, including the British Isles. At the left, across the sea, he drew the coast of the New World as he imagined it to be. He painted it green, the color map makers used to show an unknown region.

The small picture is a copy of the oldest map of the New World, made in 1500 by Juan de la Cosa. The large nautical chart was made in 1424. The red rectangle, marked Antilia, *may have been the West Indies, the North American mainland— or just an imaginary island. The blue rectangle above it may have been Greenland.* ▶

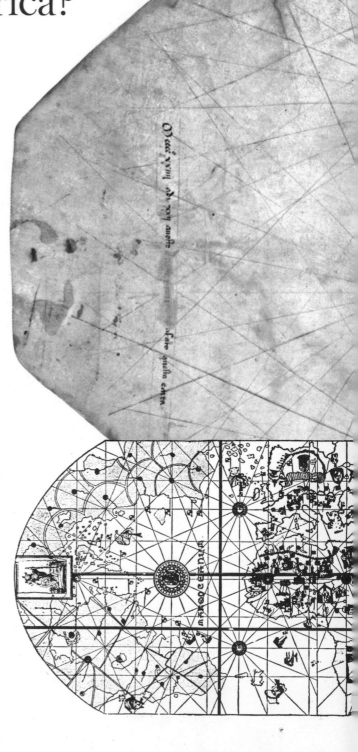

Before Columbus crossed the Atlantic, sailors believed the sea was full of fearful monsters.

La Cosa had little knowledge of the Gulf of Mexico and the Caribbean. And so he neatly covered that part of the New World with a picture of St. Christopher, the patron saint of travelers, carrying the Christ Child.

Like Columbus, La Cosa believed that the New World was Asia. Not until 1507 was the newly discovered land called America. The name was used by the German geographer Martin Waldseemüller to honor Amerigo Vespucci, an adventurer who had sailed across the ocean and claimed to be the first man to have reached the mainland of North America.

As time went on, however, Columbus was recognized as the discoverer of America, even though he had only landed on an island. Much later, scholars learned that Norsemen had reached America in the year 1000. But the Norsemen had not stayed, and they had done nothing in America to change the history of the world. Could there have been other discoverers, like the Portuguese navigators who roamed the seas before 1492?

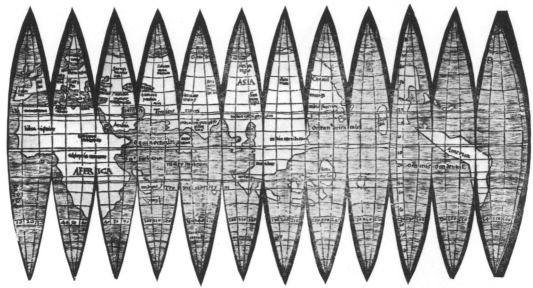

The New World was first called America in 1507 on this map. The name was used to mark Brazil, shown at the right. Made by Martin Waldseemüller, the map was designed to be pasted on a ball to form a globe.

Then, only a few years ago, a Portuguese nautical chart was found in England. Made in 1424, it shows the North Atlantic, with a red rectangle marked *Antilia.* Was Antilia a real island, or was it an imaginary one? If it was real, it could only be part of the New World—the West Indies or the mainland of North America —for the chart shows no other land west of the Azores. And if Antilia was part of the New World, America must have been discovered by Portuguese navigators years before Columbus.

Unfortunately, there is no real proof that the Portuguese ever reached Antilia. Perhaps some day the answer will be found on some old, lost map, or in the pages of a dusty manuscript. The New World has long been explored and mapped and charted. But new worlds of forgotten facts still remain to be discovered in the sea of history, and the search for knowledge is an adventure that will never end.

A painting of Columbus by Sebastiano del Piombo.

British Museum. Kodachrome courtesy Harold McCracken

The Secret Life of the American Indian

Ever since the early days of America, the white man's idea of the Indian has been changing. Sometimes the Indian seemed to be a Noble Red Man, a child of nature. At other times he seemed a bloodthirsty savage, or a lazy good-for-nothing. Today all three ideas keep turning up. Movies, books, comics, and television usually picture the Indian as a savage who lived in a tepee, wore a feathered war bonnet, and hunted buffalo on a swift horse.

And so, to most people, the real life of the Indian is still secret and hidden. For the truth is that there were many different kinds of Indians, and each led a different kind of life, spoke a different language, and dressed in a different way.

At the time the white man first came to America, there were probably no more than a million Indians scattered over what is now the United States. In the Northeast were the hunters and farmers of the woodlands. They knew nothing of the tepee. Most of them lived in wigwams—buildings of timber covered with bark, and shaped like a dome or a cone. The Iroquois, who called themselves the people of the "Long House," built huts about a hundred feet long. The huts had bunks along the sides, and a row of fireplaces down the middle.

In the Southeast, the Indians were farmers, although they did some hunting and fishing, too. Their houses had thatched roofs, and their settlements were so large that white men called them towns.

An Indian town of the 16th Century in what is today North Carolina. The Indians at the lower right are taking part in a feast ceremony. ▶

12

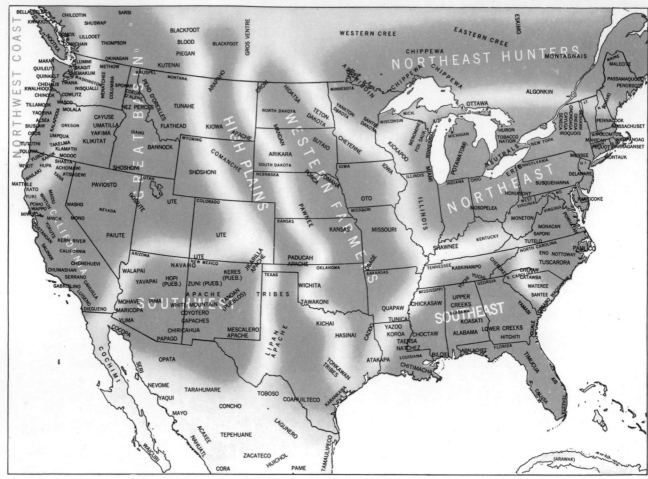

This is where the Indian tribes lived in 1650, shortly after the white man came to North America.

Even among the Indians of one region there were sometimes different customs. While most of the southeastern tribes were ruled by head chiefs, the Natchez of Mississippi had a king called the Sun. Under him were the Nobles, the Honored Ones, and the ordinary people, who were known as Stinkers.

All the southeastern Indians were warlike. But the farming Indians of the Southwest liked peace. They lived in pueblos— villages of houses built of a clay called adobe, or of stone held together with adobe. They were fine weavers and potters. In the Southwest there were also fierce tribes like the Navahos and the Apaches, who made a business of war and raided the pueblos. In time, some of them, too, turned to farming. The Navahos became artists and weavers, although they did not give up raiding.

On the Northwest Coast, the Indians had such good hunting and fishing that they did not bother to farm. They fished for everything in the water from whales to salmon, and hunted deer, mountain sheep, and other animals. They were surrounded by forests of good lumber, and made all sorts of things from wood and bark. They used wood for houses, chests, dishes, spoons, canoes, and boats, and were highly skilled carvers and woodworkers. Chiefs would place poles with carvings of their ancestors in front of their houses. These carvings came to be known as totem poles.

The people of the Northwest were ruled by chiefs, and often went on raids to capture slaves. When a chief wanted to show his greatness and riches, he would invite another chief to a feast called a potlatch. He would give his guest gifts, such as copper disks and blankets of mountain sheep wool, which were especially valuable. He might even destroy some of his goods and kill a few of his slaves.

Then it was the other chief's turn. His feast had to be larger, and he had to destroy or give away double the amount of riches. If he could not do this, he was finished as a chief. And if he could do it, he might be ruined anyway, by having too little left over for himself.

There were other Indians with different customs in the West, in the mountains and on the prairies. They were farmers or hunters. They lived in lodges covered with earth, or in wigwams covered with bark or straw mats.

But where were the Indians who roamed the plains, who lived in tepees, and shot down buffalo from swift horses? There were none. True, some western tribes did hunt the buffalo. And they did live in tepees while on their hunting trips. But hunting buffalo was hard and dangerous work without horses or rifles—and the Indians had neither.

It was the white men who brought about the great days of the Plains Indians, which began around 1722. From the white men the Indians got their horses and firearms. They quickly learned to ride and shoot. Then the white men started to drive the eastern tribes out of the woodlands.

Westward, carrying muskets, went the Chippewas, pushing the Dakotas and the Sioux into the plains. And into the plains

A Minnetaree chieftain, Pehṛiska-Ruhpa, leading the Dog Dance, a ceremony of war in which the dancers ate raw meat like wild dogs. This picture was painted in 1833 by Charles Bodmer, a young Swiss artist.

The tepee of the Plains Indians, a tent made of buffalo hide and poles, could be quickly set up or taken down.

From Red Man's America by Ruth Murray Underhill: © 1953 by the University of Chicago

to follow the buffalo went the Blackfeet and the Cheyenne, the Iowa and Comanches, the Arapaho, the Crows and the Piegans. The horse, the rifle, and the buffalo gave them a new kind of life. They ate meat the year round. They moved from place to place, carrying their tepees. They had a wonderful time, feasting, hunting, roaming, playing. But by 1880 the buffalo were gone, and the great days were over.

Again it was the white men who brought about the change, by slaughtering buffalo and driving the Indians off the land. But more than the life of the Plains Indians was changing. Before the coming of the white men, many tribes were already on the road to civilization—their own kind of civilization. Some had democratic ideas of government, which were later studied by thinkers in both Europe and America.

As time passed, the Indians found themselves living in the white men's world, and they had to change to suit the white men's ways. No longer could they move forward to their own kind of civilization.

One of the most interesting groups of Indians were the tribes of the eastern

Snake and Sioux Indians on the warpath.

Gilcrease Institute of American History and Art. Tulsa.
Photograph by Eliot Elisofon, courtesy Life

The wigwam was made of thatch or bark over a framework of poles.

woodlands that spoke the Iroquois language. Around the middle of the 15th century they were fighting among themselves instead of against their enemy, the Algonkians. They were in danger of being wiped out, when five tribes—the Mohawks, Oneidas, Onondagas, Cayugas, and Senecas—formed the League of Five Nations. They became known as the Six Nations after they were joined by the Tuscaroras of North Carolina.

The two men who did most to start the league were Deganawidah and Hiawatha, and a legend grew up about them. It told of Deganawidah, a prophet or holy man, who was sent to earth to bring peace to the nations. Deganawidah was born among the Hurons, on the northern shore of Lake Ontario. He heard of the wars of the Iroquois people, on the other side of the lake, and thought much about them. As he thought, he seemed to see before him a Tree of Peace, and the roots of the tree were the Iroquois nations. Above the tree was the Eagle That Sees Afar, on guard against enemies.

And now Deganawidah knew that the Iroquois must make peace. They must all get together and have the same laws. And they must have the might and power to see that their laws were obeyed, and to fight off their enemies.

"Peace and Power," Deganawidah said. "That is the message I will bring to the nations."

A young Indian girl of the plains swings from the branch of a tree.

18

The Bull Dance of the Mandan Indians, celebrating the coming of the buffalo.

Crossing to the other side of the lake, he reached the country of the Onondagas. They were ruled by Atotarho, a cruel chief with a crooked mind and a crooked body, whose head was covered with snakes instead of hair.

Soon Deganawidah came to the house of one of Atotarho's men. This man was a cannibal, an eater of human flesh. Deganawidah climbed to the roof of the house and looked through the smoke-hole. Below him the cannibal was putting some-

thing into a large pot that hung over the fire. Deganawidah watched as the man peered into the pot to see if the water had started to boil.

The man stared, for in the water he saw a face looking up at him, a strong and kind face. The man did not know that it was Deganawidah's reflection. He believed the face was the reflection of his own, and he was troubled.

"This is not the face of someone who kills his fellow men," he said.

19

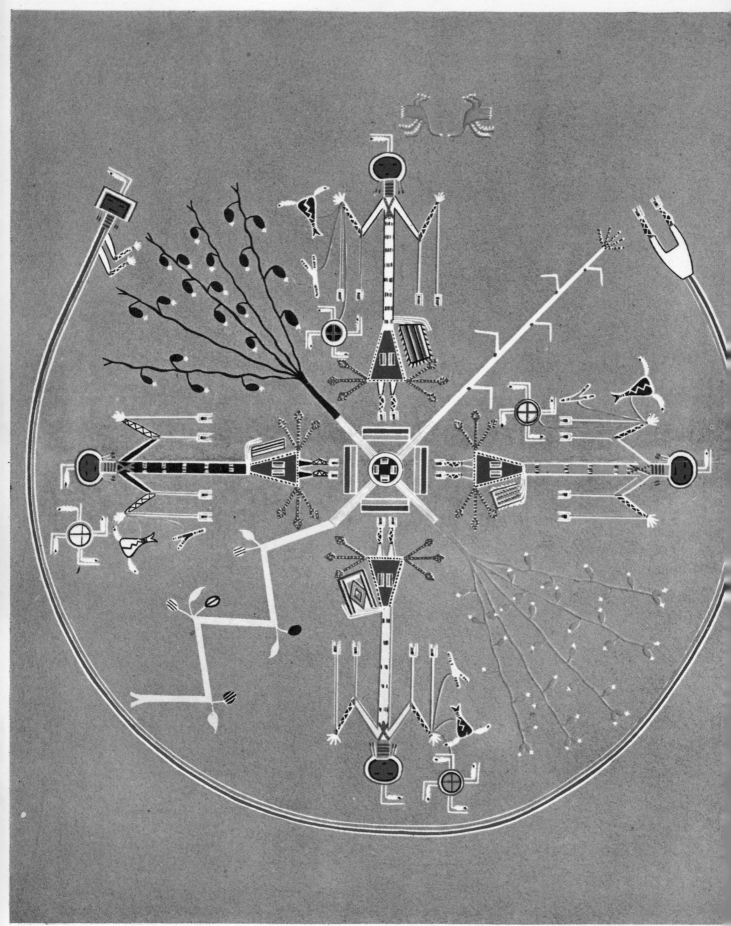

This Navaho sand painting was used in a disease-curing ceremony in the 1880's. The stick figures running diagonally from the center of the picture stand for the four yays, or gods, of corn, beans, tobacco and pumpkins. The long figure encircling most of the painting is the goddess of the rainbow. She is holding out her hands, in which the medicine for the patient was placed. A dozen artists worked eight hours to complete the picture. After being used in the ceremony, the painting was destroyed.

A pueblo, or village, of the Southwest.

He wanted to stop being a cannibal and live a life in keeping with the kind face he had seen in the water. He emptied the pot, and Deganawidah came down from the roof and stood before him. The man listened to Deganawidah's message of Peace and Power.

"It is a good message," he said. "Tell me what to do."

"Help spread the message among the nations," Deganawidah said. And he named the man Hiawatha, which means He Who Combs.

"For you shall comb the snakes out of Atotarho's hair," he said.

Deganawidah left the house and went eastward to the land of the Mohawks. Meanwhile, Hiawatha worked among his own people, the Onondagas, until one day Atotarho drove him away. He journeyed to Deganawidah in the land of the Mohawks, who had, in the language of the Indians, "taken hold" of the message of Peace and Power.

Together with the Mohawks, the two men set out to speak to the other nations. The Oneidas and the Cayugas took hold of the message at once. But before the Senecas would listen, Deganawidah had to put the sun out for a time and bring darkness upon the earth.

Then Deganawidah and Hiawatha led the Mohawks, Oneidas, Cayugas and Senecas against Atotarho. The crooked chief saw the power of so many warriors and agreed to make peace. And Hiawatha combed the snakes out of Atotarho's hair.

After that, Deganawidah planted the Tree of Peace on the shore of Lake Onondaga. And on its top he placed the Eagle That Sees Afar, to guard against enemies.

This legend became almost the Bible of the Iroquois. It helped keep them united and powerful for many years. But at last, like the other Indians, they, too, had to change, and their old life became secret and hidden to most Americans.

A stone "warrior pipe" of the 16th Century.

An Apache basket.

21

◀ *Mato-topa, a well-known Mandan chief, in a shirt of mountain sheep hide, trimmed with the hair of slain enemies. It was much like a modern soldier's decorated battle jacket.*

A Seneca crooked-face mask, used to drive out disease.

Museum of the American Indian,
Heye Foundation

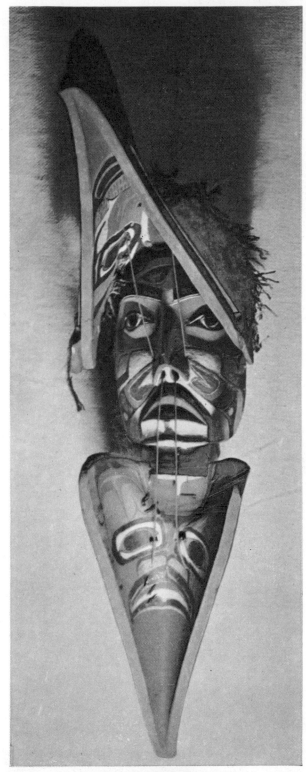

(Right) A Kwakiutl mask, four feet high, made by Indians on the Northwest Coast. With the visor lowered, it looked like a raven. (Below) A cradle of red cedar wood. The decorations include a shark and a wolf.

Frank Smith Collection, Vancouver; from Art of the Northwest Coast Indians, by Bruce Inverarity, 1950. Courtesy University of California Press

23

La Salle, the Lakes, and the Mississippi

The illustrations accompanying this article are from the Catlin Collection of The American Museum of Natural History, New York. Photographs by Herbert Loebel

The explorers dragged their equipment around Niagara Falls to a place where they could build a ship.

On a November day in 1678, a young French nobleman in a red cloak stood on the shore of Lake Ontario in Canada. He was Robert Cavelier, Sieur de La Salle, commander of nearby Fort Frontenac and owner of a large tract of land on the St. Lawrence River. With him were Count Frontenac, governor of Canada, and some Frenchmen and Indians. They were watching a boat set sail—the first boat of La Salle's expedition to find a way to the Mississippi and explore the great river.

Ahead of La Salle were years of hard-

The first boat of La Salle's expedition set sail from the shore of Lake Ontario in Canada.

ship, danger, and adventure. They would end with France the ruler of still more land in the New World, and with La Salle dead. But on this day he was full of hope.

A few months later he left to join his companions at a point on the Niagara River. His own boat was wrecked, and he was forced to finish the journey by canoe. The men of the expedition dragged their equipment around the mighty Niagara Falls, to a place where they could build a ship. All winter they worked, while Seneca warriors watched and frowned and spoke in low voices among themselves.

Supplies ran out, and La Salle went back to Fort Frontenac, walking 250 miles

through the snow of the forest and over the ice of Lake Ontario.

There were many things to keep La Salle busy at the fort. His enemies were saying that his plan to explore the Mississippi was a foolish one, and that he would never return. He had borrowed money for the expedition, and the lenders were taking his property in the settled part of Canada away from him.

La Salle was not with his men when, in the spring, they launched the *Griffin*, the ship they had built. But early in August he again joined the expedition, and they sailed off on Lake Erie, where a ship had never sailed before.

Griffin to take the furs to Niagara, leaving them there as payment for the money he owed. The ship was to return at once to Lake Michigan.

On a wild, stormy night the *Griffin* hoisted sail, while La Salle and fourteen of his men went on in canoes. Battling hunger and bad weather, they reached the mouth of the St. Joseph River, where they built a fort. They went on again, down the Illinois River. At an Indian village they were given a feast. Following their custom, some of the Indians picked up bits of food with their hands and placed them in the mouths of their guests. Others rubbed the feet of their guests with bear's grease. La Salle made the Indians a gift of hatchets and tobacco. He told them he had come to protect them and to teach them to pray to the true God.

Near the village, La Salle built another fort, naming it *Crevecoeur*—Heartbreak. Then the party split up and La Salle returned to Canada for more supplies. He learned that the *Griffin* had never reached Niagara. It had gone down somewhere on the lakes.

Months went by—months of more journeyings, of hardship and fighting with the Indians. Many of La Salle's men deserted. Again he had to raise money and buy supplies. He had to recruit new men. But at last he started south again, in the dead of winter. The streams were frozen, so he placed his canoes on sledges and dragged them over the ice.

Then the party reached open water on a branch of the Illinois River, and launched their canoes. And on the sixth of February,

On the Erie, the St. Clair, the Huron, La Salle sailed, over waters that spread before him like a sea. Then he turned westward into Lake Michigan, where he anchored near one of the islands at the entrance of Green Bay. Here he picked up a large store of furs from several members of his advance party. He ordered the

27

Feasting with the Indians on the Illinois River.

1682, they floated into the Mississippi. Down the river they went, past the mouth of the muddy Missouri, while the air grew warmer and warmer with spring. In March, at the mouth of the Arkansas River, they put up a cross and visited with the Arkansas Indians.

As they made their way along the rolling waters, they visited other tribes—the Taensas, the Natchez, and the Coroas.

Only once were the Indians unfriendly, and the canoes floated on and on, until La Salle and his men reached the end of the river, and saw a vast gulf of blue salt

Pulling canoes on sledges over the ice and snow.

On the Mississippi River, the expedition stopped at the mouth of the Arkansas and put up a cross.

water, heaving under the blue sky above.

On April 9, 1682, La Salle assembled his men. He raised a cross and the banner of France, and in the name of the most high, mighty, invincible, and victorious Prince, Louis the Great, by the Grace of God, King of France and of Navarre, he took possession of the great land which he called Louisiana.

(Next page) Dressed in a white robe, the chief of the Taensas Indians greeted La Salle. While the chief spoke, his wives howled to do him honor. ▶

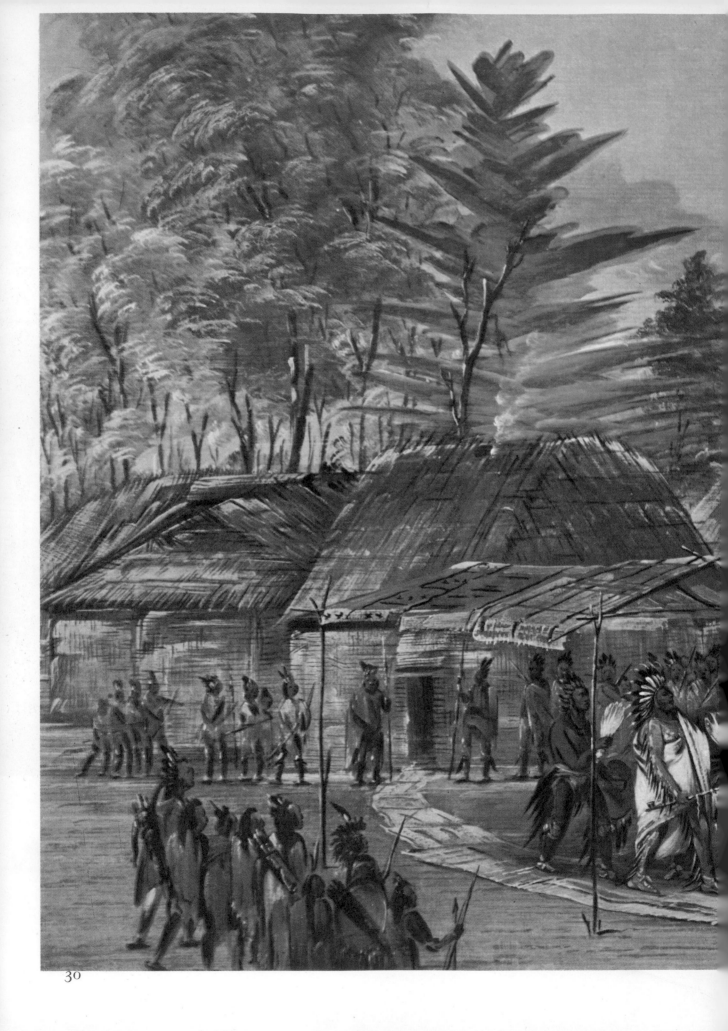

Reaching the end of the Mississippi and the Gulf of Mexico, La Salle claimed the territory of Louisiana for France.

This was not the last of La Salle's adventures. In 1684 he led an expedition of 400 men from France to start a colony at the mouth of the Mississippi. One of his four ships was taken by the Spanish, and in the West Indies he became sick with a fever. He sailed too far westward, missed the mouth of the river, and two of his ships were wrecked on the coast of Texas.

La Salle went ashore, still trying to find the Mississippi. Some of his party wandered off, others died of starvation or sickness. When only forty-five men were left, he decided to march to Canada—a journey of 2,500 miles through the wilderness. This was too much for the men, and on January 7, 1687, several of them ambushed and killed him.

Standing over La Salle's body, one of the murderers cried out, "There thou liest, great Bashaw! There thou liest!"

And the men wandered off, leaving La Salle to the buzzards and the wolves.

On another expedition, from France, two of La Salle's ships were wrecked on the Texas coast.

*Still searching for his lost river, La Salle went on shore,
where he was killed by several of his desperate men.*

Highwaymen of the Seas

The pirate Blackbeard got his name from the "large quantity of hair, which, like a frightful meteor, covered his whole face." He always tried to look as fierce as he could. He wore a scarlet silk sash, six pistols, lighted matches under his hat, and often carried a two-foot knife between his teeth.

Samuel Bellamy, pirate, was talking to the captain of a ship he had just captured, plundered, and sunk. He apologized for the sinking, which had been done by the crew against his orders. Then he said:

"Tho', damn ye, you are a sneaking Puppy, and so are all those who will submit to be governed by Laws which rich Men have made for their own Security, for the cowardly Whelps have not the Courage otherwise to defend what they get by their Knavery; but damn ye altogether; Damn them for a Pack of crafty Rascals, and you, who serve them, for a Parcel of hen-hearted Numskulls. They villify us, the Scoundrels do, when there is only this Difference, they rob the Poor under the Cover of Law, forsooth, and we plunder the Rich under the protection of our own Courage; had you not better make One of us?"

Bellamy used strong language, even for a pirate. But many other men, especially Americans, did not think too badly of pirates in the early part of the 18th Century. At that time, Americans were still colonists ruled by kings in Europe. They could not trade as they wished. Piracy was, after all, just one more way of getting around unjust laws.

Not that capturing and robbing ships at sea was anything new. There had been pirates among the seafarers of Phoenicia, and of Greece and Rome. The Barbary pirates of the northwest coast of Africa had worked at their terrible trade for many centuries, and would not be wiped out until 1830. And there were many pirates in the waters around the British Isles.

It was privateering that made the pirates almost respectable. A privateer was a man with his own ship who was given permission by his government to capture enemy ships. If he could bring an enemy ship into port, he was given the largest

Pirates were loyal to no country, and flew this black flag of death and terror from the masts of their ships.

share of the ship and its cargo. If he was too far from a port, he could take the cargo and sink the ship.

Privateering was profitable as well as patriotic. One of the first privateers was an Englishman, Sir Francis Drake. Queen Elizabeth gave him permission to capture Spanish ships and raid Spanish lands in America. Drake brought back to England treasure worth about 1,500,000 pounds in English money.

Later, during King William's War and Queen Anne's War, American seamen from New England and the middle colonies became privateers. And when the wars were over, they hated to give up their free, adventurous life. The ordinary work of the sea seemed too tame. Besides, it did not pay enough. Times were bad in the colonies, and earning an honest living was not easy. And so many American seamen ran up the Jolly Roger—the pirate's black flag with white skull and crossbones. They turned from lawful privateering to unlawful piracy, and became highwaymen of the high seas.

English pirates, too, were at work along the American coast. During Queen Anne's War, they had attacked the rich Spanish

(Next page) The rich town of Santo Domingo, in what is today the Dominican Republic, was attacked in 1585 by Sir Francis Drake. The map shows his ships at anchor in the harbor, and his men battling outside the city walls. Drake was given permission by Queen Elizabeth to attack Spanish ships and lands, but many people believe that what he did was piracy. ▶

CIVITAS S Domingo sita
in Hispaniola Indica Angliæ mag:
nitudine fere æquali, ipsa vrbs eleganter ab Hispanis extructa, et omnibus
circumimentie insulis vera dat.

36

Nec Spe Nec Metu

Captain Bartholomew Roberts, an outstanding pirate of the 18th Century, once captured eleven ships with only two of his own.

ships in the Spanish Main—the seas around Spain's lands in South America. They knew that the islands and inlets and coves of the American coast were the best of hiding places for their ships. And they came to America for another reason, that had to do with rum and trade and patriotism. American merchants in the northern colonies did a big trade in rum, making it of molasses from the islands of the West Indies. But the law was that they must trade only with islands owned by Britain, and they could not get all the molasses they needed.

As time went on, the laws became more strict. To stay in business, the merchants were forced to break the laws. They also felt that it was their patriotic duty. They were Americans, and should not have to obey laws made for them in England. Some day this would lead to war against Britain and the start of a new nation, the United States of America. Meanwhile, the merchants got molasses and other goods by smuggling. And they did not mind doing business with pirates.

In New York City, for example, the merchants carried on trade with pirates

Anne Bonny and Mary Read were two of the few women who became pirates. They were known as fierce fighters.

who had their headquarters at Madagascar, an island off the coast of Africa. The pirates even visited New York, first bribing the governor and other officials so that they would not be arrested. They were friendly with rich and poor. They sold their loot at bargain prices, and told exciting tales of their adventures.

In 1696 Captain William Kidd, a sea captain of New York, was sent out by a new governor to capture "Pirates, Free Booters, and Sea Rovers" wherever he might find them. For three years he sailed in his ship, the *Adventure Galley*. He returned with treasure, part of which he buried on Gardiners Island off Long Island. But the story had spread that he himself had turned pirate. He was arrested, taken to England, and put on trial.

Captain Kidd swore that his men had mutinied, made him prisoner, and turned his ship into a pirate craft. Few people believed him, and he was hanged for murder and piracy. For years tales were told and songs were sung about him, and he became the most famous pirate in his-

tory. But had he been a pirate at all? No one really knew.

But there was never any doubt about Blackbeard. His real name was Edward Teach. He was called Blackbeard because of his long, coal-black whiskers, which he wore in fancy braids. Between capturing ships, he hid at places along the coast of North Carolina. He shared his loot with the governor of North Carolina, and had nothing to fear until he began to attack ships from Virginia.

The governor of Virginia sent a ship after him, and Blackbeard was killed in a bloody battle. His head was cut off, put on a pole, and carried ashore at Hampton, Virginia.

This happened in 1718, and piracy soon died out on the coast of the American colonies. But the pirates have not been forgotten. To this day, some people believe part of Captain Kidd's treasure is still buried on Gardiners Island. And in Hampton, Virginia, there are those who say that the headless ghost of Blackbeard still walks at night.

The New World Changes Warfare

A 17th-Century musketeer, armed for battle, obeys the command: "Charge your pike at the right foote and draw your sword."

The first English settlers who landed at Jamestown in 1607 were ready for battle. Like most European soldiers, they wore armor—breastplates to protect their chests, light metal skirts to protect their legs, and helmets on their heads. They carried a strange collection of weapons. Besides their matchlock muskets, they had pikes, poleaxes, and swords. All of these were still used in European warfare.

The musket proved to be their best weapon against the Indians, even though it was hard to handle. It weighed fifteen pounds, was six feet long, and had to be propped up on a rest before firing.

To load the gun, the musketeer first poured a charge of black powder into the muzzle and dropped in a two-ounce lead ball bullet. Then came wadding, rammed down with a long iron ramrod.

The firing mechanism was the match-lock, a metal clamp that held in place a slow-burning fuse called the match. When the musketeer pulled the trigger, the fuse dropped into a small pan of priming powder outside the barrel. The primer caught fire, and the flame passed through a touch-hole in the barrel, setting off the powder charge. With a roar and a cloud of smoke, the bullet was sent out in the general direction of the enemy.

With their weapons and armor, the settlers brought from Europe strict rules of warfare. Battles were always fought on open, level stretches of country, by two armies facing each other in straight lines. If the weather was bad, there would be no fighting, because muskets could not be fired in the rain. A battle was like a game—a deadly game in which men were killed and wounded, but which was always played according to the rules.

In the wilderness of the New World, things were different. There were few open, level stretches. Instead, there were hills and valleys and thick forests. And the Indians did not fight by the rules. Many a settler found, as did Captain Underhill of Connecticut, that the Indians would not fight "openly in ye feeld" when he "chose to beat up the drum and bid them to battle." He complained that "none would come near us."

The Indians fought from cover, hiding behind rocks and bushes and trees. Their men did not form straight lines, but spread out through the woods. They made surprise attacks, often swooping down on a settlement and then disappearing into the dark forest.

Musketeers follow instructions in the use of the matchlock musket, a complicated weapon. Right: "Charge your peece." Below, left: "Give fire." Below, right: "Hold your musket in your rest and with the left hand onely in Ballance."

From Maniement D'Armes, published by Jacques de Geyn in 1608

(Next page) Illustration shows how battles were usually fought in Europe. Here, the armies of King Charles I and Sir Thomas Fairfax face each other, ready for battle. In the center of the line, *each infantry regiment is made up of a battalion of pikemen between two battalions of musketeers. At the ends of the line are cavalry troops. Sir Thomas Fairfax is pictured at upper right.* ▶

THE DESCRIPTION OF THE ARMIES OF H

Sr Thomas Fairefaxe his Excellency, as they were dra

the Fowerte

Dust Hill

Prince Rupert

Prince Maurice

Sir Barnard Astley

His Perso

The King

The Left Way Commanded by
Cornett Generall Ireton

Maior General Skippon

Forlorne hope
Musquetiers

Coll:

Coll: Vermidens
commanded by Maior
Huntington

Maior General
Ireton

Maior Generall

Coll: Rosser Rege:ment

Coll: Pickrod Regiment

Right Hill

Fanny Hill

The Mill Hill

Lieutenant Coll: Prise a
Reserve

Loure leafe hill

The traine guarded with firelockes

NASBYE

AND FOOT OF HIS MAJESTIES, AND
erall bodyes, at the Battayle at NASBYE;
of June 1645.

Prince
Regiment   Ruperts of foote

Colonell   How
ar.tr.   horse

The   Lord   Bard
       Terlia

Sir George Lisle
             Terlia

Sir   Marmaduke Langdale and The Nasarbe horse

The Generall

Coll Mountague gues
              The Generalls Regt

The right wing of horse commanded
By Lieutennant generall Cromwell

Coll Whallyes Regt   Sir Robert the
                           general deuision of
                           the life guard

Coll Hamm ond a Re forue
      Coll Raynsboro ugh Reforue

Coll Shuffialds de maſter   Coll the Vins

The Reserue horse

Coll Vines   Coll the Reſ.ter

place this mapp between fol 52 53

43

Painting by J. L. G. Ferris. Reproduced by special permission of the owner, Glens Falls Insurance Company

The rules of warfare changed in the wilderness of the New World.
This is the battle of Rogers' Rock, fought by Major Rogers' Rangers
against the French and Indians near Lake George in 1758.

After some bitter defeats, the settlers began to fight like the Indians. They gave up armor and pikes and swords, and began to use knives and hatchets. They wore heavy leather or quilted cloth coats. Their guns were improved, becoming lighter and easier to handle. They forgot the Old World's rules of battle, and learned new ways of warfare in the New World.

Soon the settlers were beating the Indians, pushing them back off the land. The white man quickly learned the lesson of forest warfare—a lesson he would never forget. It was one among many he had to learn in the strange new world called America.

44

The Yankees
Take Louisbourg

The Essex Institute, Salem, Mass.

Sir William Pepperell.

"Fortified towns are hard nuts to crack," said Benjamin Franklin in a letter to his brother. "But you seem to think that forts are as easy taken as snuff."

The year was 1745, and Britain was at war with France. The war had spread to the American colonies, and now the New England Yankees were set on attacking the Fort at Louisbourg in French Acadia. From Massachusetts and New Hampshire, from Connecticut and Rhode Island came the Yankees, 4,000 of them. They were farmers, fishermen, shopkeepers, carpenters, blacksmiths—volunteers with little military training.

And Louisbourg was one of the great forts of the world. It had taken twenty-five years to build, at a cost of $6,000,000. Some of its walls were thirty feet high and forty feet thick at the base. Guarding it were two outerworks, with batteries of cannon. No, Louisbourg would not be "as easy taken as snuff."

But the Yankees would not give up their plan. They did not trust the French, and Louisbourg stood for the might of France and its king, Louis. Who knew when the French might decide to sweep down upon New England and swallow up the British colonies? Sooner or later the French had to be put in their place, and this was as good a time as any. Louisbourg must fall.

And so the Yankees started off in a fleet of sixty ships, under the command of William Pepperell, a merchant of Maine. They took with them cannon and ammunition, including some 42-pound cannonballs. These cannon balls were too large for the guns on the ships, but they would fit the guns in the fort's outerworks. The big guns could then be turned on the fort itself.

Luckily, the Yankees had a small number of men who knew how to handle

Next page: The landing of New England troops at Louisbourg in 1745. ▶

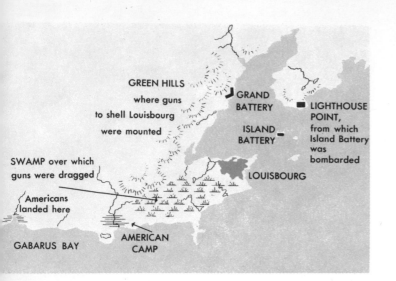

GREEN HILLS
where guns
to shell Louisbourg
were mounted

GRAND
BATTERY

LIGHTHOUSE
POINT,
from which
Island Battery
was
bombarded

ISLAND
BATTERY

LOUISBOURG

SWAMP over which
guns were dragged

Americans
landed here

AMERICAN
CAMP

GABARUS BAY

Map of Louisbourg, showing location of the fort and its outerworks, and the points where Yankee guns were placed.

cannon. They also had gunsmiths and blacksmiths who could make repairs and keep the guns in working order. All would be needed in the battle.

On April 30 the Yankees landed on Cabarus Bay, driving off a small French force. Colonel William Vaughan led his regiment inland, where he came across several unguarded storehouses of naval supplies. He set them afire. Clouds of smoke, black from tar, pitch, and oil, drifted down on one of the outerworks, called the Grand Battery. The next morning he found that its 400 French soldiers had fled, scared off by the smoke screen. They had left behind powder and shot and twenty heavy cannon.

The joyful Yankees turned the guns on the French and started a bombardment. They did not worry about ammunition, for now they could use the 42-pound cannon balls they had carried in their ships.

But the other outerwork, the Island Battery, was still not taken, nor was the great fort itself. Cannon had to be brought ashore from the ships, on clumsy flatboats through the roaring surf. And then they had to be dragged more than two miles to the hills overlooking the fort. Over sand and rocks the men pulled the

cannon, mounted on carriages. Then they came to a swamp, where carriages and guns began to sink down in the mud.

While they paused, wondering what to do, the cannon of the fort opened fire on them, forcing them to take cover.

Then they set to work making wooden sledges. A cannon was placed on each, and teams of 200 men pulled the sledges across the swamp. Gun by gun, in fog or night to escape French gunfire, they brought their cannon to the hills. Teams of 300 men even hauled five of the captured French 42-pounders through the sticky mud.

Then the French and the Yankees fired at each other. The month of June came, and the bombardment was still on. The Yankees tried to capture the Island Battery, but were thrown back with a loss of 189 men. They hoisted cannon up the steep cliff of Lighthouse Point, dragged them a mile and a quarter, and trained them on the Island Battery. The gunfire was so fierce that Frenchmen ran out and dived into the sea.

Day after day the big guns roared and thundered—and at last the white flag of surrender flew from the great fort. The Yankees were happy, but their happiness did not last long. When the peace treaty was signed, Britain traded Louisbourg back to the French in exchange for Madras in India. In 1758, when another war came, the fort had to be taken all over again.

The trade of Louisbourg became one more reason for the Yankee colonists to dislike the British government in London. But they had learned that they could fight, and fight bravely and well.

Daniel Boone, Hero

Boone's powder horn.

Daniel Boone was one of the greatest of American pioneers. But, like many other pioneers, he was not much of a hand at writing. For example, on the stock of his rifle he carved these words: *Boons best FREN*. And once, after killing a bear, he carved on a tree: *D Boone killa bar on this tree 1773*. The world might never have known Boone's story if he had not met John Filson, a schoolmaster.

Boone told his adventures to Filson, who wrote them down in what he pretended were Boone's own words. Filson's book was published in 1784. Within a few years it was reprinted in London, and translated into German and French. Boone became a hero to Europeans. They thought of him as a man who had turned away from civilization and found happiness in living close to nature.

This old print, drawn from the artist's imagination, shows Boone protecting his family.

Eli Whitney's Magic Machines

There was a kind of magic in Eli Whitney's machines, a strange kind of magic he could not control. One of his inventions changed the South, and helped bring on the Civil War. Another changed the North, helped it win the war, and started America on the way to becoming a great industrial nation.

Even as a boy, Eli Whitney loved to tinker with mechanical things. He was born in Massachusetts in 1765, and grew up on his father's farm. He spent more time puttering in the workshop than doing chores. He could repair anything his neighbors brought to him, and to earn money he manufactured nails, hatpins, and walking canes.

After graduating from Yale at the age of twenty-seven, Whitney went South. He had been offered a job as a private tutor for a family in Georgia. But when he got there, he was told that someone else had already been hired.

Luckily, on the trip down by boat, he had met Mrs. Nathaniel Greene, the widow of the Revolutionary War general. She had asked him to stay for a while at her plantation in Savannah, and now he accepted her invitation. Mrs. Greene soon found that there was nothing Whitney could not make or mend, and she was delighted with his "handiness."

One day some friends of Mrs. Greene called on her. They were officers who had served under her husband, and they owned plantations in the neighborhood. As usual, they began to talk about the hard times in the South. The world needed cotton, but they could not afford to grow it. The reason was that there was no quick way to separate cotton from its seed. A slave had to work ten hours to clean one pound of cotton.

No, it did not pay. Why, there was hardly any use keeping slaves these days! It might be a good idea to set them all free. If only someone could invent a machine to clean cotton cheaply and easily!

"Gentlemen," said Mrs. Greene, "tell your troubles to Mr. Whitney. He can make anything."

This Currier & Ives print shows slaves working in the fields of an old-time cotton plantation.

51

They did tell their troubles to Mr. Whitney, and within two weeks he had invented the cotton gin. It was a simple machine. A revolving drum dragged the cotton through a wire sieve. The seeds remained behind, and a revolving brush swept them into a container. The gin could clean as much cotton in one hour as several men could clean in a day.

Whitney tried to keep his invention a secret until he could get it patented, but word of it got out and his workshop was broken open. The gin was easy to copy, and before long it was in use all over the South. More and more cotton was planted. In two years the amount of cotton the United States sold to other countries rose from 138,000 to 1,601,000 pounds.

Before the cotton gin, slavery had been slowly dying out in the South. But now cotton was king, and the king needed slaves to work in the fields. Plantation owners stopped talking about freeing the slaves and bought as many as they could.

Whitney made very little money from his invention. He returned to the North and began manufacturing guns by a new method. Instead of using highly skilled men to make individual guns, he had unskilled men make parts that could be put together to form complete rifles. The parts were interchangeable. They were cut from a pattern by a milling machine he invented, and could fit any rifle.

Other manufacturers began to use Whitney's milling machine and his

Slaves using a cotton gin—a machine that changed American history.

(Above) An old painting of Eli Whitney's gun factory near New Haven, Connecticut. (Below) Some of the guns made by Whitney.

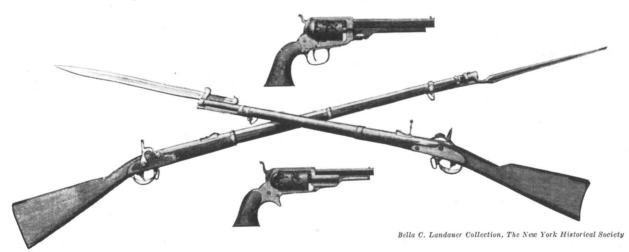

method of interchangeable parts. It was the start of mass production—making goods in great quantity by machine.

Whitney died in 1825, but his machines went on working their magic. The North became a land of industry, and needed free workers for its factories and shops. The South was farming country, with cotton its one big crop, and needed slaves.

Something had to change, and the change was decided by a great war. The North won, partly because its factories kept turning out rifles, uniforms, boots, and other equipment as fast as they were used up.

And so it came about that the machines invented by Eli Whitney changed history, and helped to shape a great nation.

53

Washington's Spy at Trenton

It was just three days before Christmas, in the winter of 1776. On the Pennsylvania side of the Delaware River, on the frozen, snow-covered fields, George Washington's army was camped.

Without tents or blankets, his men sat huddled around open campfires. Half of them had no shoes, and all of them were hungry. They did not need to be told that several days ago Washington himself had said, "I think the game is pretty near up." They had almost been destroyed on Long Island and at White Plains. They had been chased across New Jersey by the British and their hired Hessians.

Now, a few miles down the river, on the other side, the Hessians held the snug little New Jersey town of Trenton. How long would it be until they struck and ruined forever America's hope for independence?

A little distance from the camp, two of Washington's soldiers were sitting on stumps under a clump of trees. Their horses stood quietly nearby. The soldiers, too, were quiet, listening to the low moan of the wind. Suddenly they saw a cow running across the fields. And running after the cow, shouting and cracking a long whip, came a man.

The two soldiers leaped into their saddles and rode toward the stranger at a gallop. For a while he held them off, slashing with his long whip. Then he slipped on a patch of ice and fell. Before he could get up, the two soldiers were upon him, pointing a pistol at his head.

The man cried out, speaking with a heavy Scotch accent. He was only a poor butcher, a cattle dealer, trying to find meat to sell to the Hessians. His name was John Honeyman.

The soldiers looked at each other. They had heard talk about a John Honeyman. He was said to be a Tory, and a British spy. Quickly they bound him with a rope and took him to Washington's headquarters.

There was a frightened look on Honeyman's face as the soldiers pushed him into the room where Washington was waiting. Washington ordered that Honeyman be left alone with him. The door closed behind the soldiers—and then a strange thing happened. Washington smiled at Honeyman, and Honeyman grinned back.

For, while it was true that John Honeyman was a spy, he was a spy for the Americans. He and Washington had set up their

This old print of Washington at the battle of Trenton is not accurate. Actually, the Hessians rushed about in confusion.

plans in Philadelphia, a year and a half before. He met twice then with Washington, who had just been made Commander-in-Chief of the Continental Army. Honeyman was usually not much for talking, but for once he spoke up. He told Washington he would do anything to free America from Britain.

During the French and Indian War, Honeyman had been forced into the British Army. On the ship coming over to America, he had saved General Wolfe, the British commander, from a bad fall. Wolfe had given him a letter, naming Honeyman his bodyguard.

With this letter, and his honorable discharge from the British Army, Honeyman could easily win the trust of the British. He would pretend to be a spy for them, while actually spying for Washington.

There was only one hitch. He was a weaver, and would have little chance to mingle with the British. And so he decided to go back to his old trade as a butcher and cattle dealer, and furnish meat to the British Army. Whenever he had important information, he would let himself be captured by Washington's men, putting up a fight so that he would not be suspected. Then he would be allowed to escape.

Washington agreed with the plan. If he ever wanted to see Honeyman, he would get word to him. No one except Honeyman's wife was to know their secret.

And so Honeyman moved his wife and four children to New Jersey, where there were many Tories. He saw Washington for the third time when the Americans were retreating toward the Delaware. Washington ordered him to stay with the British Army and find out all he could.

And now the general and his spy were meeting for the fourth time. Honeyman gave a careful report of what was happening in Trenton. Washington listened closely. When he had retreated across the Delaware, to keep from being followed, he had taken every boat in sight. Were the British building more?

Honeyman was able to tell him that no boats were being built, nor were any being brought in from other towns. Colonel Rall, commander of the Hessians, had no fear of Washington's "army of farmers." His thoughts were on the big celebration the Hessians were planning for Christmas.

After Honeyman finished telling what he knew, Washington called a sentry. He ordered Honeyman held in the guardhouse for court-martial the next day.

But late that night the spy's guard ran off to help put out a fire that broke out in a haystack. The guardhouse door was mysteriously unlocked, and Honeyman escaped. A bullet from a sentry's gun whistled past him as he plunged into the darkness. He crossed part of the Delaware River on the ice, waded the rest of the way, and at last, tired and wet, he reached Hessian headquarters.

He told Colonel Rall of his capture and said he had escaped by breaking a window. He had picked up some important information. Washington's army was close to mutiny. Rall nodded and smiled. Just as he thought, he had nothing to fear. He would go ahead with his plans for the Christmas party.

On the other side of the river the next morning, Washington seemed furious when he was told of Honeyman's escape. But that same day he sent a message to his officers: *Christmas day at night, one hour before day, is the time fixed for our attempt on Trenton.* And his men began to prepare for the attack.

Christmas day came, and the Hessians had their celebration. That night, as Colonel Rall sat playing cards and drinking, a Tory farmer pounded on the door.

Word had got out that the Americans were getting ready to move. A servant refused to let Rall be interrupted. The farmer quickly wrote a note, warning that Washington's men were on the way. Rall stuffed it into his pocket without reading it, and went on with his game.

Early in the morning, a sleet storm came up. Rall and most of his men, heavy with food and rum and wine, slept through it. But Washington had already crossed the Delaware. His troops, marching barefooted or with rags around their bleeding feet, stormed down upon the town.

In less than an hour, the battle was over. Rall lay dead, shot as he tried to rally his men. The Hessians lost 106 dead or wounded, and 812 were captured. Only four Americans had been hurt. It was the first big American victory of the war, a victory badly needed, and it put new heart into Washington's fighting farmers.

As for John Honeyman, his days as a spy were not yet over—and neither were his troubles. Twice he was jailed by American patriots and faced death for treason and aiding the enemy. Both times he was freed in a mysterious way.

But at last peace came, in 1783, and John Honeyman returned to his home. One day his daughter Jane was sitting on the porch of their house. All through the war she had been hurt and puzzled by the things her neighbors said about her father. Now she looked up in surprise as Washington and a group of American officers rode into the yard. And, while a crowd of neighbors watched, Washington shook hands with John Honeyman and thanked him for what he had done for his country.

Honeyman lived to the age of ninety-three and became a well-to-do farmer. He said little about his work as a spy, and after his death he was all but forgotten.

Then, years later, the world learned the

story of how he and Washington had given the nation one of the most important victories in the war.

And today, on the New Jersey side of the Delaware, at the place where Washington's army landed, there stands a stone fountain with these words:

DEDICATED IN MEMORY OF
JOHN HONEYMAN
WHO SERVED WASHINGTON AND
THE CONTINENTAL ARMY
AS A SPY

DRINK OF THE FOUNT OF LIBERTY
LET POSTERITY INHERIT FREEDOM

57

Charles Willson Peale, who taught his whole family to paint, himself painted this portrait of Alexander Hamilton, first Secretary of the Treasury.

pictures had been good, Peale might never have thought of becoming a painter himself. But they were very bad, and he was sure he could do better. When he returned home, he began to paint. He found that he could make money at it, and decided to make painting his trade.

Peale took lessons from John Hesselius, paying for them with one of his best saddles, and from John Copley in Boston. Then, in 1766, eleven wealthy men of Maryland sent him to London to study with Benjamin West, a well-known artist. Peale was already a patriot who wanted the colonies to break away from England. He refused to take off his hat when King George passed on the streets.

Three years later Peale was back in America. He traveled through Virginia,

The
Patriot Painter

Charles Willson Peale was a painter, and the brother, father, uncle, and teacher of painters. He and his family painted many pictures of George Washington and other famous Americans. But he never even saw a painting until he was a grown man.

Peale was a saddlemaker in Annapolis, Maryland, and did watchmaking and silversmithing on the side. One day he went to Norfolk for leather supplies, and there he saw paintings for the first time. If the

Rembrandt Peale, son of Charles Willson Peale, painted the portrait of Robert Fulton, inventor of the first successful steamboat.

58

John Paul Jones, the American naval hero, was painted by Charles Willson Peale around 1781, after Jones had won a great sea victory.

Independence Hall Collection; Courtesy Time Inc.

Maryland, Delaware, and Pennsylvania, painting portraits as he went. In 1772 he visited Mount Vernon and made the first known portrait of George Washington. In the years to come Peale would paint many more pictures of Washington, for the two men liked each other. Peale had only one complaint. Often, while he was painting, Washington would fall asleep.

When the Revolutionary War started, Peale took his family to Philadelphia. He was made captain of a company of volunteers and fought at Trenton and Princeton. He was brave enough, but a little unusual for a soldier. He carried paints and a palette as well as a musket. If his men were hungry, he would cook them a meal. If their boots wore out, he made them fur-lined moccasins. And if he had nothing else to do, he painted miniature pictures of the officers.

Peale believed anyone could learn to paint, and he taught painting to everyone in his family—brothers and sisters, sons and daughters, nephews and nieces, and other relatives. He had seventeen children, and two of his sons, Rembrandt and Raphaelle, became famous painters.

There was always something doing at Peale's house, for he was interested in politics, music, nature, science, and mechanical things as well as art. He even tried his hand at inventing. He made fiddles, xylophones, gunpowder, shoes, eyeglasses, and false teeth. He kept live bears, birds and snakes, an elk, and a five-legged cow with two tails.

The New York Historical Society

Thomas Jefferson was a lifelong friend of the Peale family. This picture of him was painted by Rembrandt Peale, whose career he helped.

Charles Willson Peale painted this earliest known portrait of Washington in 1772.

Rembrandt Peale was only seventeen when he painted this picture of Washington.

Washington looked more heroic in a later portrait by Rembrandt Peale.

In this portrait of Washington by the elder Peale, the captured Hessian flags at the right and the college buildings and prisoners in the background stand for Washington's victories at Trenton and Princeton.

In 1801 Peale heard of the discovery of a few bones of a huge, prehistoric animal on a New York farm. He raised some money, borrowed equipment from the Army and Navy, and started off on the first scientific expedition in America. He dug up two full skeletons of the mastodon, and later painted a picture of the digging.

By this time Peale had a collection of pictures of Revolutionary heroes, painted by himself and his family. He also had, besides the mastodon skeletons, a collection of birds, animals, and reptiles which he and his family had mounted and stuffed.

Peale decided to open a museum. As the collection grew, he moved it to Philosophical Hall and then to the second story of Independence Hall. There were about 100,000 items in the museum, including displays of minerals, insects, and all branches of natural history—and the trigger finger of an executed murderer. Washington sent him some pheasants, Benjamin Franklin sent a French Angora cat, and Jefferson gave him some specimens that had been brought back by the Lewis and Clark expedition.

Many of Peale's ideas were far ahead of his time. He believed that all men were created equal; he hated slavery, and freed the slaves he had inherited. He never spanked his children, and thought that girls as well as boys should be educated.

He also believed that if men took care of themselves properly they could live to be 112. He himself went on working well into his old age. In his late seventies he improved on a new invention, the velocipede, an early form of bicycle. Soon his whole family were traveling on velocipedes through the streets of Philadelphia.

Peale often went to Washington, visited the White House, and painted a number of famous people. At eighty-one he learned

This is part of a picture showing Peale's scientific expedition to dig up the bones of a mastodon. He painted himself at left, holding his drawing of a mastodon leg. His wife Hannah is just behind him.

a new style of painting from his son Rembrandt, who had just returned from Europe. He painted one of his best-known pictures, *Christ Healing the Sick,* and two years later painted his own portrait.

When Peale reached the age of eighty-six, it looked as though he might indeed live to be 112. But one day, in the middle of the winter of 1827, he did something that could have killed a man half his age. Cold and tired, he carried a trunk on his back for a whole mile, just to save a little time. The strain on his heart was too great, and he lived for only several months after that. But even as he died he was studying his own pulse.

And so ended the long, happy, useful life of Charles Willson Peale. Some of the people who knew him called him a boy who never grew up, and perhaps he was. He never lost his curiosity and his joy of living. But he was also a man of ideas and a patriot. In his own way he helped to make history, and he left behind paintings that are a record of the days when America was young.

The Great Sea War

The paintings accompanying this article are reproduced through the courtesy of Irving S. Olds, with the assistance of Harry Shaw Newman.
Photographs by Herbert Loebel

Oliver Hazard Perry, a hero of the War of 1812, was twenty-eight when he won the battle of Lake Erie. The flag behind him carries the words of another naval hero, James Lawrence: "Don't give up the ship!"

The Constitution *and the* Guerrière.

Much of the War of 1812 took place on the water, and the wooden sailing ships that fought the sea battles will be long remembered. Long remembered, too, will be the captains who commanded the ships—men like Oliver Hazard Perry, James Lawrence, Stephen Decatur, Isaac Hull, William Bainbridge, David Porter, Jacob Jones, and Thomas Macdonough.

The United States had only sixteen ships against the British Navy's 800, but its three frigates—the *Constitution*, the *President*, and the *United States*—were faster and better than any of Britain's vessels. Most of the battles in this war were duels between single ships. The ships fired their guns at close range, and the sailors often fought hand-to-hand with cutlasses.

The most famous ship was the 44-gun frigate *Constitution*, shown above as she fought the British ship *Guerrière*. She was built of live oak and red cedar, with bolts from Paul Revere's shop, and carried about 450 men.

On August 19, 1812, the *Constitution* and the *Guerrière* met off Halifax, 600 miles east of Boston. Captain Isaac Hull, who commanded the American craft, waited until the two ships were very close before he gave the order to fire.

Then, time after time, the *Constitution*'s guns roared out, toppling the *Guerrière*'s masts, ripping holes in her hull, and killing and wounding seventy-nine British sailors. The *Constitution*'s own hull stood up so well against the enemy's cannon balls that her crew gave her the nickname "Old Ironsides." In thirty minutes the battle was over and the British surrendered. The world was amazed to hear that the young American nation had won a victory over the finest navy on the seas.

63

The Constitution *won another great victory on December 29, 1812, when she sank the British frigate* Java *off Brazil. The four pictures at the right show how the* Java *was destroyed. The* Constitution *closed in (1), shot down the* Java's *masts (2), leaving the vessel helpless (3). The British then surrendered, and after the crew was removed, the* Java *was blown up (4). These pictures were made from sketches done on the spot by a lieutenant in the British Navy.*

(1)

(2)

Early in the war, the Constitution *was becalmed in the midst of a British squadron. She made her escape when her men towed her with small boats and hauled on the line of an anchor dropped ahead until she found a breeze.*

(3)

(Next page) The battle in which the British frigate Shannon *captured the U. S. ship* Chesapeake *in fifteen minutes on June 1, 1813. As the wounded American captain, James Lawrence, was carried below during the battle, he said the famous words: "Don't give up the ship!"* ▶

(4)

This diagram shows the movements of the Constitution *and the* Java *in their famous battle. The guns could be fired from the side only, so each captain tried to cross the bow of the other ship. Then he could fire across the enemy's deck without danger of being hit himself. The* Constitution *crossed the enemy's bow about eight times.* ▶

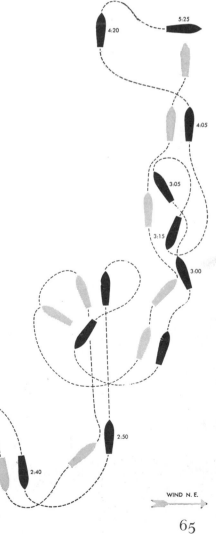

5:25

4:20

4:05

3:05

3:15

3:00

2:50

2:40

TIME—2:10 P. M.

JAVA

CONSTITUTION

WIND N. E.

Stephen Decatur

Americans had less reason to cheer in 1813, when the U. S. ship *Chesapeake* was captured by the British frigate *Shannon*. The loss of the *Chesapeake* was a bitter blow to the Americans, but there was a reason for her defeat. Most of her officers and men were new to the ship. They needed more training to be able to sail the ship, man the guns, and carry out orders during battle. But the chance for that training never came.

Still, Americans could not forget the victories of the *Constitution*, and the triumph of another frigate, the *United States*, over the British ship *Macedonian*. On October 25, 1812, Stephen Decatur, captain of the *United States*, captured the *Macedonian* and brought her into New York.

Strangely enough, Decatur did not fight again until after the war was over. He was bottled up in New York harbor by the British fleet, and could not break out and go to sea until January, 1815. By that time a peace treaty had been signed by Britain and the United States, but the news had not yet reached Decatur. Sailing on the frigate *President*, he came across four enemy ships. He escaped from three of them and defeated the fourth, the *Endymion*. Later he was caught by the other three ships and forced to surrender.

The Chesapeake *was brought into Halifax with the white ensign of Britain flying over the flag of the United States.* ▶

The United States *captured the British ship* Macedonian *in 1812.*

On Lake Erie, Commodore Perry's Niagara *pushed through the British line to win the battle and gain control of the lake for the United States.*

Two of the most important naval battles of the War of 1812 were fought, not on salt water, but on the fresh water of the Great Lakes. And in both battles young American officers defeated an entire British squadron.

At the beginning of the war, the Americans thought they could easily take Can-

ada. But the army was badly prepared and got nowhere. In 1813 the British still held Canada and controlled Lake Erie. In the spring of that year, a young naval officer was sent to Erie, Pennsylvania, with orders to build a fleet of ships and lead it against the enemy. He was Commodore Oliver Hazard Perry, and in September his fleet

A second British fleet was defeated a year later by Commodore Thomas Macdonough, who captured seven ships in a battle on Lake Champlain.

was ready to leave Put In Bay. There were nine ships in all, and Perry was aboard the brig *Lawrence*, flying a flag that read: "Don't Give Up The Ship."

On September 10, Perry met a British squadron and opened fire. The *Lawrence* was soon wrecked by British cannon balls and put out of action. Taking his flag, Perry transferred to another of his ships, the *Niagara*. He sailed through the enemy line, his cannon blasting away at the British. After a fifteen-minute bombardment, the British surrendered. Perry then sent General William Henry Harrison a message that became famous: "We have met the enemy and they are ours."

Young Perry's victory gave the United States control of Lake Erie. It allowed General Harrison to cross the lake and attack the British on the Thames River in lower Canada.

The following year, on September 11, 1814, another British fleet was defeated on Lake Champlain. The Americans were led by Commodore Thomas Macdonough, who was only thirty years old. His victory, coming at the same time that the Americans were winning a battle on land, helped to turn back a British attack from Canada.

Under heavy fire, Perry transferred from his own wrecked ship to the Niagara. *His twelve-year-old brother, a midshipman, rode beside him in the stern.*

Major General Andrew Jackson became a national hero after his great victory at New Orleans.

Culver Service

Old Hickory at New Orleans

General Andrew Jackson stared at the man who stood before him in his headquarters at New Orleans.

"You say the British fleet is at Lake Borgne?" he asked.

"Yes, sir."

Old Hickory, as Jackson was called, had been waiting for news of the enemy for a long time. The War of 1812 was in its third year and had become a kind of guessing game. For several months there had been no sign of the British. In August, 1814, they had attacked and burned Washington, in September they had struck at Baltimore, and then they had sailed away. No one knew when or where they would strike next.

It was Old Hickory's job to protect the cities of the South along the Gulf Coast.

His forces were pretty well spread out. Some of his troops were stationed near Baton Rouge, others were near Mobile, 200 miles away.

Now that he knew the British were at Lake Borgne, Old Hickory had to make still another guess. Did the British really plan to attack New Orleans? Or were they trying to trick him into gathering all his forces at New Orleans while they sailed away and struck somewhere else?

Thinking it over, he decided that the British were planning to attack New Orleans. He sent for his troops at Baton Rouge and Mobile, but many days passed without further word of the enemy. Then on December 23, 1814, Jackson learned that the British were just eight miles below the city.

That night, after darkness had fallen, the U. S. war schooner *Carolina* slipped quietly down the Mississippi River. She anchored close to the bank, opposite the campfires of the British. Old Hickory's army, marching along the side of the river, came up as the *Carolina* opened fire with her big guns. The Americans closed in and struck hard with bayonets, tomahawks, hunting knives, and fists. After two hours of fighting, a heavy fog rolled in, and Old Hickory drew back with a number of prisoners.

From them he learned that the British had a force of 10,000 hardened veterans. Jackson had about 5,000 men, many of them volunteers from the backwoods of Tennessee, Kentucky, and Mississippi.

Old Hickory was no student of military science. But he understood backwoodsmen, for he was a backwoodsman himself. He knew they were among the best shots in the world. And yet he was sure that in an open battle they would not be able to stand up against the well-trained British. The Americans were used to fighting from behind trees, like the Indians.

And so he ordered his men to dig trenches behind the Rodriquez Canal, several miles below the city. The wet soil was so hard to handle that they built walls of cotton bales to protect themselves.

The British advance guard made a small attack on December 28. A few days later, on January 1, 1815, they brought up their cannon and pounded the Americans with shot. The bales of cotton caught fire. Pieces of the burning stuff flew through the air, almost setting fire to the Americans' ammunition.

Major General Pakenham led the British at New Orleans. He died on the field of battle.

Some of the burning bales fell into the canal and sent up a thick screen of smoke. For a time the Americans were blinded and could hardly see the enemy. But again the British were thrown back, leaving some of their cannon behind.

Old Hickory ordered his men to get rid of the dangerous bales of cotton. They dug in with their shovels, built up a strong embankment of earth, and waited for the British. And on January 8 the British came. The redcoats fixed bayonets and marched forward, keeping perfect step, as though they were on parade.

At first there was only silence from the muddy brown earthworks where the Americans stood. Then their cannon and the long rifles of the backwoodsmen spoke up. Many of the redcoats fell, leaving big gaps in the British lines. Then the British re-formed and marched on, ripped and blasted by American fire.

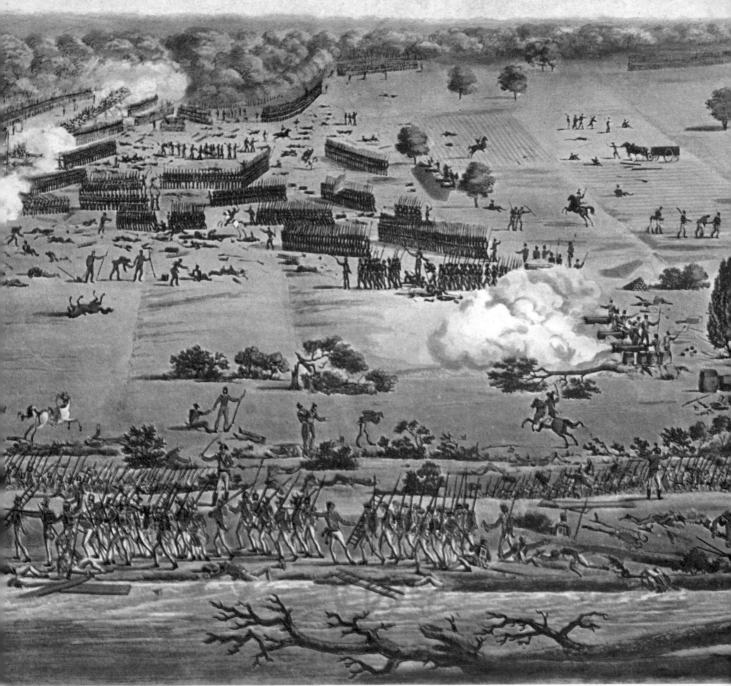

Mabel Brady Garvin Collection, Yale University Art Gallery

In less than twenty minutes the British fled, after losing 2,000 men. General Pakenham, their commander, was killed. Only eight Americans were killed and thirteen wounded.

The battle took place two weeks after the peace treaty had been signed in Ghent, Belgium, but the news had not yet reached Jackson. The victory made Old Hickory a national hero, and he was elected President in 1828.

This view of the Battle of New Orleans is taken from an old engraving. At left, Old Hickory (standing near the American flag) and his army are dug in behind an embankment five feet high. The American line of defense went from the left bank of the Mississippi River to a cypress swamp a mile and a half away. The British redcoats are carrying ladders to lay across the canal. At this early stage of the battle, the British were already being mowed down. By the time the battle ended, 2,000 of them were killed or wounded, compared to twenty-one American casualties.

75

Made for America

In the early days of the United States, Americans liked to display decorated chinaware on their shelves and tables. Not much chinaware was made in America, and most of these bowls, pitchers, and plates came from foreign lands, such as China and England.

American ships sailing to China brought

back many objects of porcelain. They were made in potteries at Ching-te-Chen and carried hundreds of miles overland to merchants in Canton.

Some of the chinaware was decorated with Chinese scenes, like the punchbowl below. It shows the *hongs*, or foreign trading stations, in Canton. But many pieces were decorated to order, or painted with pictures that the Chinese thought would be liked by Americans. Sometimes the artists copied American coins, the seal on a ship's papers, or a sketch made by a sea captain. Or, like the English craftsmen, they would paint famous Americans they knew little about. They wanted to satisfy their customers, and they did.

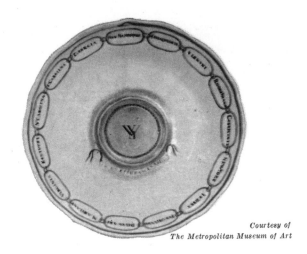

This saucer was part of a dinner service given to Martha Washington. It carries her monogram.

The coat of arms of New York State is painted on this tea caddy, made in China.

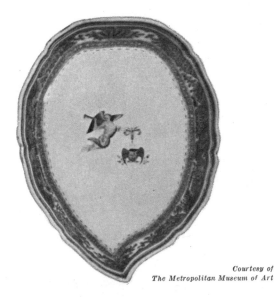

A dinner service presented to George Washington included this richly decorated pickle dish.

77

These plates came from the famous potteries at Staffordshire in England. After
the War of 1812, the English made many
such plates decorated with American
scenes. They copied the pictures from illustrations in books. This pottery was
popular with Americans until around the
end of the Civil War.

The plates shown above depict the New
York City Hall and the landing of the
Pilgrims at Plymouth Rock. The plates
below show Harvard College and the
President's House, Washington.

The city of Liverpool in England was a
center of pottery as well as a seaport.
When American ships began to come to

English pottery makers decorated jugs and pitchers like those at right with hand-painted designs of sailing ships. The tea set below, made at a later date, is decorated with a view of a steamboat.

Liverpool shortly after 1783, its potteries turned out cream-colored earthenware with special designs for Americans.

Many jugs, pitchers, and bowls, like those shown above, were decorated with designs of ships. Some of the designs were actually of English ships, but American flags and other details were added to make them more suitable for buyers in the United States. American heroes, such as Lafayette, Decatur, Washington, and Franklin were also pictured, and scenes of American naval victories were popular.

The tea set below was made in the early 19th Century, and was decorated on one side with a view of Fulton's steamboat, the *Clermont*. On the other side was a picture of a sailing ship supposed to be the *Cadmus*, which brought Lafayette to America for a visit in 1824.

Even the fine porcelain factories of France made pieces for the American trade in the early 1800's. They, too, carried special designs painted by skilled artists. And so it came about that many homes in the United States had on their shelves plates, jugs, pitchers, and bowls not made *in* America, but made *for* America.

Salem's Ships Sailed East

(Above) The seal of the City of Salem. It shows an East Indian carrying a parasol, with palm trees and a ship in the background. The Latin motto reads: "To the farthest port of the rich East."

(Below) A wharf in Salem. The picture was painted in 1805, when Salem's merchants carried on heavy trade with the East Indies.

Farming was hard in New England, and many a New Englander left his plow to seek his fortune on the sea. The men of Salem, a small town in Massachusetts, were no exception. At first they were fishermen, going far out to the Grand Banks for codfish. Then they began sailing

The paintings accompanying this article are from the collection of the Peabody Museum of Salem

their trim little schooners south to the West Indies, exchanging codfish and lumber for sugar, salt, or molasses. Often they went to ports on the Mediterranean, and once in a while to the coast of Africa.

When the Revolution came, the men of Salem went out in larger ships, called privateers, to attack the ships of Britain. And when the Revolution was over, Salem was left with a fleet of 158 privateers. These vessels were too large for the West Indies trade. Besides, Britain ruled the West Indies, and Americans could no longer do business there. And so Salem sent its ships to the East—to China, and India, and the lands of the East Indies.

And Salem sent its sons, too, farm boys from the surrounding countryside. Some of them were as young as fourteen. They turned up at the wharves, in their hands a small bag of belongings, and in their heads such advice as: "If you meet the Devil, cut him in two and go between the pieces."

To the eager boys, the smell of the wharves—of spice and tar and rope and salt water—was the smell of fortune and adventure. And, indeed, there was adventure ahead on the long voyages. Salem's ships often stopped to buy pepper at Sumatra, a tropical island of white sand, palm trees, and towering green peaks. Malays in their bright sarongs would come smiling from their huts—when they did not turn pirate and try to murder captain and crew.

Flags of Salem's ships and merchant houses, painted about 1835.

Some ships cruised among the islands of the South Pacific, with their cannibals and headhunters and laughing girls. Here the crews hunted for the *bêche-de-mer*—a kind of sea worm, which was later sold in China to flavor soup.

In China itself there were the strange sights of the city of Canton, where the river was jammed with ferryboats, canal boats, sampans, barges, junks with eyes painted on their prows, and flower boats with tinkling music. And there were sights just as strange in the cities of India, in Calcutta and Rangoon and Madras, or the hot places of the African coast.

There was money in sailing, too. In the

early days of the Salem voyages, each seaman was given space on the ship to carry his own goods for trading, such as a few kegs of tobacco or some large New England cheeses. Captains could take as much as five tons of goods. Besides their wages, captains were paid from one to eight per cent of the profits of the voyage.

Small fortunes were made by young captains like Nathaniel Silsbee. He and his two brothers commanded ships before they were twenty. By the time they were thirty, they had left the sea and set themselves up as merchants.

One of the largest fortunes in Salem was made by a man who never went to sea at all. He was Elias Hasket Derby, a merchant with the nickname of "King" Derby. He knew ships and trade and what was going on in the world, and he became America's first millionaire.

The years between the Revolution and the War of 1812 were the greatest for Salem. Its warehouses were crammed with the treasures of the East—silks from China, coffee from Mocha, sisal from Manila, painted cloth from India, ivory and gold from the coast of Africa. Its merchants built splendid mansions on Chestnut Street, and in their rooms were rare and beautiful things brought from across the sea.

Few days passed without a ship coming in. Young lads who had never even seen the nearby city of Boston would walk down the gangplank, full of tales of strange and distant lands. In their sea chests were souvenirs of far places—an elephant's tooth, perhaps, or a goblet carved from the horn of a rhinoceros.

During the War of 1812, Salem again built privateers. But when the war was over, only fifty-seven ships were left from its fleet of 200. More ships were built, and once again trade was good. Joseph Peabody was the leading merchant, just as "King" Derby had been before him.

Then, in the 1820's and '30's, America began building larger ships. They were too big for the shallow water of Salem's harbor. Slowly more and more business went to Boston, and the merchants closed

In ships such as this, Salem's merchants did business with distant lands. The bark Patriot, *built in 1809, was used in both the Baltic and East India trade. The picture shows her off the city of Copenhagen.*

The worst disaster in the history of Salem took place in 1902, when the ship Ulysses *and two others were driven onto Cape Cod by a blizzard. Eighty-seven seamen from the three ships froze to death.*

Sometimes they swapped tales of the distant seas, or watched the arrival of a coastwise lumber schooner. And when the sun began to go down, they walked slowly through the shadows down Chestnut Street, past the mansions of the old merchants, and they found it hard to say what was dream and what was real.

Today the mansions of Chestnut Street still stand. In the Peabody Museum is one of the world's finest collections of Oriental objects, and row on row of the sea journals of captains long dead. They are reminders of the time when Salem's ships were on the seas, sailing to the farthest ports of the rich East.

their warehouses and wharves and moved away. The years went by, and only a few old shipmasters were left. They dozed in the sun before the big, drafty Customs House, dreaming of the great days that were no more.

The waterfront of Canton, China, in the days of Salem's trade with the East. The flags of Denmark, Spain, the United States, Sweden, and Great Britain fly over the hongs, *or trading posts, where foreigners did business.*

Buffalo Hunter, *painted about 1840 by an unknown artist.*

Painters of the West

The first white men who came to America found the New World a world of wonder. It was a big land, with great green forests, vast open prairies, tall mountains, enormous rivers. And the Indians, the people of this land, were just as strange as the country around them.

As white men filled the East, pushing back the wilderness for their settlements and towns and cities, the West remained a place of wonder. Easterners wanted to know what it looked like, how its plants grew and its animals behaved, how its rivers ran and where its mountains rolled.

And so, in the 19th Century, exploring parties and government expeditions set out to learn all they could about the West. And with them went artists, to make a record of the West in pictures. Like the unknown artist who painted the buffalo hunter shown above, they took a long look at the Indians as well as at the land.

Many of the artists came from Europe, and were trained in England, Germany,

85

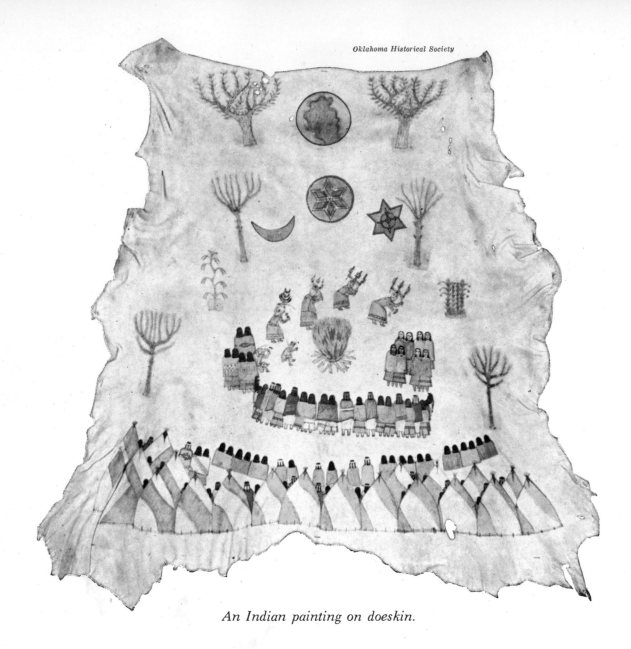

An Indian painting on doeskin.

Austria, or France. Some of them roamed about on their own, going as far west as they could, often joining with traders and trappers. Others were sent by magazines to give eastern readers a view of the land of cowboys and Indians.

Time brought great changes to the West. Farther and farther, over plains and mountains, stretched the wires of telegraph lines and the tracks of railroads. These things, too, the artists painted, for it was their job to set down the life of the West on paper and canvas. But they still felt the wonder of the land, and they put

that wonder in the pictures they painted.

The white men were not the only artists of the West. Long before they came to America, the Indians were making works of art. Sometimes they did paintings on animal skins, like the doeskin painting above. This one was made by an Apache chief named Naiche, who was second in command to the famous Geronimo.

Naiche used a soft buffalo bone for a brush, and vegetable dyes for paints. The picture shows a dance around a fire during a religious ceremony. The figures wearing the large headdresses are medicine men.

*An Indian village scene
painted by George Catlin.*

George Catlin was born in Wilkes-Barre, Pennsylvania, and for two years was a lawyer in Philadelphia. Then he began to study art, and in 1832 he went west to paint the Indians.

For thirty years he traveled in Indian country, painting such pictures as *A Sioux Village* (above) and *A Buffalo Chase* (below). He made hundreds of paintings of Indian Life, many of which are now in the National Museum, Washington, D.C. The American Museum of Natural History, in New York, has about 700 of his sketches. Catlin lived with Indians in both North and South America and learned their languages and customs.

Catlin understood the Indians and the excitement of the buffalo hunt.

Albert Bierstadt was born in Germany and was brought to the United States when he was about a year old. At the age of twenty-three he went to Germany and studied painting for three years at Düsseldorf. He returned to America, and during the 1850's and 1860's he roamed the West. He painted Indians and buffaloes, wagon trains, and the Rocky Mountains, which he loved more than anything else.

Experts in painting did not care too much for his pictures. But most people liked them, and one of them sold for $35,000, the highest price that had ever been paid to an American painter.

When he painted The Last of the Buffalo (right), there were still great herds on the plains. Within a few years they had been wiped out, not by the spears of Indians, but by the guns of the white hunters.

The Corcoran Gallery of Art

International Business Machines Corp.

In this picture, titled The Rocky Mountains, *Bierstadt captured the beauty and majesty of the high country in the West.*

Hubert Blazza

The paintings on pages 87-93 and 95 are reproduced through the courtesy of McGraw-Hill Book Company, Inc., from Portrait of the Old West *by Harold McCracken*

The Indians of the West fascinated European painters like Karl Bodmer, who did this scene, entitled Interior of a Mandan Hut.

89

Karl Bodmer was a Swiss painter who went up the Missouri River in 1833 with Prince Maximilian of Wied-Neuwied, a German explorer and scientist. Bodmer painted Attack on Fort McKenzie *after he saw a war party of* Crees and Assiniboins attack the camp of the Blackfeet outside the fort.

Assiniboin and Yankton Indians.

A battle between Indians and troops was depicted in The Silented War Whoop *by Charles Schreyvogel.*

Seth Eastman was an army officer. He spent ten years in the Sioux country, where he painted many pictures of Indian life. They include this picture of the Sioux playing the game the French called lacrosse.

No artist ever caught the spirit of the West as faithfully as Frederick Remington. The land, its people, its animals—he loved them all.

Frederick Remington was an easterner who studied art at Yale and in New York City. In 1880, when he was nineteen, he went west to become a cowboy and gold prospector. Instead, he began filling notebooks with sketches of men and animals. They were the first of the more than 2,700 paintings and drawings he completed. He was a sculptor and writer as well as a painter, and he became widely known.

Once Remington said he wished to be remembered as someone who knew the horse. But pictures such as *Attack on the Supply Train* (above) and *Friends or Enemies?* (left) show that he knew much more than the horse. He also knew the Indian, the cavalryman and the cowpuncher, the wagon train, the roundup,

and the campfire. They were all part of the Old West, which had already begun to disappear in the years when Remington was painting it.

93

In 1866 Francis Palmer drew this imaginary scene of a wagon train (left). But the West, like the rest of the nation, was changing fast. One of the men who saw it change was Charles M. Russell. He was a cowhand in Montana for twenty years, and painted *Trail of the Iron Horse* (above). It shows a band of Indians gazing at the railroad track that meant the end of their way of life.

By the 1880's, when Henry F. Farny painted *The Song of the Talking Wires* (below), there was a line of telegraph poles across the buffalo range. The Indians had been pushed off their lands and forced to live on reservations.

The Song of the Talking Wires, *painted by Henry F. Farny.*

How They Killed the Buffalo

Early settlers and travelers in the Great Plains of the West thought there were enough buffalo to last forever. In 1832 Captain Benjamin Bonneville reported, "As far as the eye could see, the country seemed blackened by innumerable herds."

Pioneers told of herds that covered fifty square miles and contained two, three, and four million buffalo.

The Indians killed only what they needed for food and clothing. But when fur traders offered money for buffalo

(Above) Stampeding buffalo could wreck a covered wagon train. Sometimes unfriendly Indians would cause a stampede for that very purpose.

(Below) There were four great buffalo herds. Their ranges overlapped because the herds moved with the seasons in search of food.

robes, they began killing the animals by the thousands. In 1848, 110,000 robes were shipped down the Mississippi.

After the Civil War, buffalo hides were used for leather, and an army of men shot buffalo for their pelts. One Kansas hunter claimed that he shot 1,500 of the animals in a week.

More than a million buffalo hides were taken out of the Kansas area in 1872 and 1873. In 1877, 1,500 hunters were at work in Texas alone. Many people wanted to stop the great slaughter. But others said it was a good thing to kill off the buffalo. Then the Indians would have to leave, and the plains could be used for cattle. So the killing went on, and in a few years the great herds were gone.

◀*(Left) A family of American buffalo. A bull weighs about 2,000 pounds, and a cow about 1,200.*

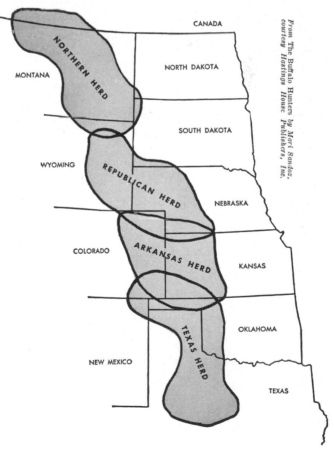

From The Buffalo Hunters *by Mari Sandoz, courtesy Hastings House Publishers, Inc.*

The Mountain Men

State Historical Society of Colorado

Like the other mountain men, Jim Baker lived by trapping beaver in the Rocky Mountains.

"Do'ee hyar now, boys? Thar's Injuns knocking round, and Blackfoot at that; but thar's plenty of beaver too, and this child means trapping anyhow."

That was Old Bill Williams speaking, and it took more than Indians to keep him from trapping beaver. For Old Bill was a mountain man, and it was beaver that had brought him to the Rocky Mountains in the first place.

The mountain men came after the Lewis and Clark expedition reported that there were swarms of beaver in the streams of the western mountains. At that time the best men's hats were made of beaver fur, and hat makers could use any number of the skins. And so in 1822 W. H. Ashley led a trading party up the Missouri, and many of the men with him stayed on.

Others followed, living in the wilderness like Indians. Besides their traps, they carried only a rifle, a knife, an awl, powder and lead. They might have a mule, or a horse or two. They ate mostly meat, from animals which they shot themselves.

Some of them lived with the Indians and took Indian girls for wives. But they were not family men. They made no settlements, no farms, no homes. For protection they traveled in small groups, or with a companion—and there were a few who hunted alone.

Once a year, in the summer, the mountain men held a rendezvous, or big meet-

Mountain men gathered for a rendezvous in the Wind River Mountains. Here they sold their furs and enjoyed themselves.

ing. Here they would sell their furs to the traders who came in wagon caravans from St. Louis. They would greet old friends, swap stories, sing, yell, gamble, drink, eat, fight. Then, when the rendezvous was over, back into the mountains they went for another long hunt.

What drew them back to the dark forests? What called them to face burning heat and freezing cold, hunger and thirst, dirt and loneliness? It could not have been the furs they sold, for no mountain men became rich. It was the life itself they loved—a wild, free, dangerous life in a free and dangerous land.

Always, there was the wonder and mystery of the land. They set their traps in secret places where no white man had been before. They floated on shining rivers in boats of skin or bark, or on rafts of logs. They rode hidden trails that wound through dim and dusky woods, between the silent, stony mountains.

They wandered as they pleased. They obeyed no law but their own. If they were sleepy, they slept. If they were hungry, they ate. If they were thirsty, they drank. That is, if there was anything around to eat or drink.

No matter what else they did, they yelled. They yelled when they fought Indians or grizzly bears. They yelled when they met strangers. They yelled when they stampeded and stole horses. They sang and shouted around their feasts at night, just to make a human sound under the great starry sky.

And they killed. They killed anything that moved, including each other, sometimes for no reason at all. Death meant little to them. More than once they would come upon the body of a companion who had been butchered by Indians. The head would be up on a stake, with the hat on, shot full of arrows. And often, when fighting Indians, they would do some butchering themselves.

Although they all lived the same life, there were all kinds among them. There were the wise and the foolish, the kind and the cruel. Most of them lived and died and were forgotten, but there were others who left their names in history—names like Kit Carson, Thomas Fitzpatrick, Jim Bridger, Jed Smith, Hugh Glass.

Famous or not, they were too strong and fiercely proud for civilization. They had no use for cities and towns. The smallest of backwoods settlements were prisons to men who knew the free life of the mountains.

And then, suddenly, in the 1840's, they were done for. First, beaver hats went out of style. The mountain men could no longer exchange their furs for the few things they needed—new traps, a knife, powder and lead. And the cold streams of the mountains no longer swarmed with beaver. Too many had been trapped in too short a time.

And even if there had been beaver, and a market for it, there was something else. Americans were on the move, pushing west to build homes and clear land for farms. Creaking covered wagons were bringing people into the wilderness, and

The Trappers' Return *shows how the mountain men floated on the rolling rivers.*

Courtesy Detroit Institute of Arts

One of the mountain men who roamed the early West is shown in this picture, called The Trapper *or* Long Jakes. *It was painted about 1844.*

with the people came the beginnings of civilization.

Some of the mountain men held out to the last, but they could not stop the rush of history. Some settled in the backwoods. Others, like Kit Carson and Jed Smith, became scouts and guides for expeditions and wagon trains of settlers. Old Bill Williams, the strange old man of the mountains, the wild hermit who walked alone —he, too, gave in. He became a guide for Charles Frémont's fourth expedition.

In spite of Old Bill's efforts, one-third of the expedition died in the terrible Rocky Mountain winter. Bill was brought into Taos, unable to walk, almost blind, frozen as high as the hips. A few weeks later he and a companion went back to the mountains, to get the expedition's baggage. They disappeared, never to be seen, never to be heard of again.

And, somehow, the story of Old Bill seems to tell what happened to all the mountain men.

101

Pathfinder of the West

West of Fort Laramie, in what is now Wyoming, the Indians were on the war-path. The trader at the fort warned Lieutenant John Charles Frémont and his party to turn back. The Sioux, Cheyenne, and Gros Ventres Indians had united to make war on the trappers. Two small parties had recently been murdered not far from the fort.

Frémont was then only twenty-nine, and that year, 1824, he was leading his first survey expedition into the Rocky Mountains. His thirty men were all armed, but they were not soldiers. Most of them were Frenchmen he had hired in St. Louis.

Kit Carson was the guide for the party, which included a map maker and a hunter to shoot animals for meat. There were also two small boys, one of them only twelve years old. They had been taken along to prove that the trail west to Oregon was safe for women and children.

One of the official reasons for this survey was to find locations where forts could be built as a protection against the Indians. Frémont had known all along that places could not be found without going into dangerous Indian country. Besides, he had orders to go as far west as South Pass, and he meant to follow them.

Some Sioux chiefs at the fort tried to make him change his mind, saying that no one could control the young Indians who were causing trouble. By this time most of the Frenchmen in the party had become frightened. They threatened to quit if he did not turn back.

Frémont became angry. He lined up his men and said that the dangers ahead were the kind they had agreed to face when he had hired them. But if there were any cowards among them, they could step forward and he would pay them off at once. The men's shame was stronger than their fear. Only one of them stepped forward, and he was jeered at by the others.

John Charles Frémont led his men through dangers and hardships. His courage won the respect of such famous scouts as Kit Carson and Alexis Godey.

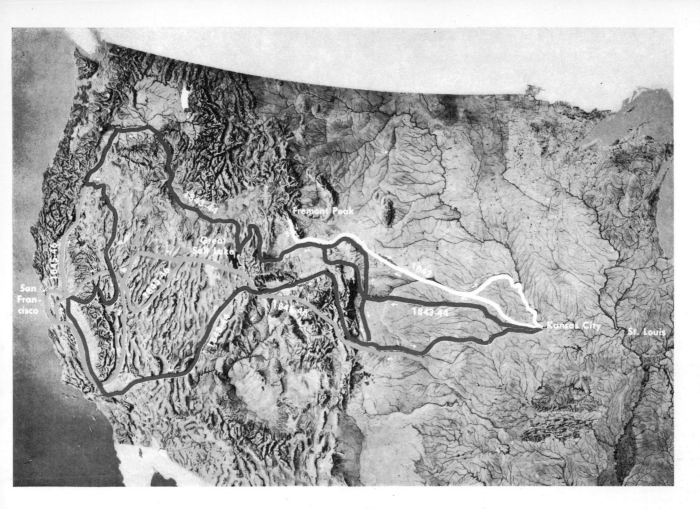

*Frémont won fame as one of the West's greatest explorers
as a result of the three expeditions shown on this map.*

In this way Frémont won the loyalty and respect of his men, and they followed him willingly the next day. The two boys were left at the fort, and the party continued up the Sweetwater Trail to South Pass—the great pass that was later to become the mountain-crossing place of the Oregon Trail.

As it turned out, Frémont saw only a few Indians on the way, and none of them gave any trouble. But he learned from Kit Carson how to stay alive in Indian country. No bright fires were allowed after dark. The horses were always kept close to camp and guarded during the night.

It was on this first expedition that Frémont climbed the great mountain in Wyoming that now bears his name. With Kit Carson as guide, he later made two other expeditions into the Far West, mapping a large area of California and the Rockies. In his journals he made notes on the weather, the elevation of the land, the kind of rocks he saw. He also took notes on animal and plant life, and wrote down many interesting observations about the Indians he met.

Frémont showed the way to thousands of settlers who traveled the long cross-country trails in wagon trains. He will always be remembered as the great pathfinder of the West.

(Next page) Towering Frémont Peak overlooks a Shoshone Indian camp in Wyoming. Frémont climbed the peak on his 1824 expedition. He wrote: "It seemed as if . . . Nature had collected all her beauties together in one chosen place." ▶

A Nosegay of Valentines

For someone as sweet as preserves.

For someone as sour as a pickle.

No one knows who sent the first valentine. Valentine's Day, February 14, is the feast day of St. Valentine. But there seems to have been nothing in the life of the saint related to the custom of sending valentines.

Perhaps the custom goes back to ancient Rome, where young men and women exchanged presents on February 14 in honor of such gods and goddesses as Pan, Juno, and Venus. Or it may have something to do with the old belief of many people that February 14 was the day on which all birds chose their mates.

In Shakespeare's time, the first girl a young man saw on that day was his valentine for the year. And the first of the couple to say, "Good morning, 'tis St. Valentine's Day," could claim a present from the other.

About 100 years ago, color printing, cheap postage, and improved mail service made valentines very popular in the United States. Some were meant just to poke fun, but most were very fancy indeed —just the thing to make a good impression on a sweetheart. Although valentines have changed over the years, they are still exchanged by sweethearts on Valentine's Day.

Around 1900, people were going in for big, fancy —and expensive—valentines like this one. ▶

106

Around 1850 a woman named Esther Howland of Worcester, Massachusetts, began making valentines like the one at the right by mass production. She and her friends put the parts together in her home on a kind of assembly line. Her business grew to $100,000 a year. ▶

The Norcross Collection

Museum of the City of New York

(Above) In this valentine, made in 1842, the earnest young man is pointing out the church to his lady love. (Right) This shy young maiden is about to send her message of love on the wind. (Below) A note written on "The Bank of Love."

The Norcross Collection

108

There were humorous
valentines, too. Some
of them made fun of
people, like these two
about the Civil War.

*Famous artists sometimes drew valentines.
The one below is by Francesco Bartolozzi.*

THE FLORIST

The side of the ship opened in this valentine.

In 1879, a young man in love might have sent this Currier & Ives print, called "The Cream of Love," to his valentine.

Built for Speed

The clippers were the swiftest sailing ships that ever put to sea, and the most beautiful. There was music even in their names —*Flying Cloud, Zephyr, Witch of the Waves, Cutty Sark.*

It was gold that brought the clippers into being. At first it was the gold from hauling cargoes of tea from China to England. Tea lost its flavor quickly when stored in a ship, and London merchants paid high prices for fast delivery. And so American shipbuilders began building clippers, in Baltimore in 1832, and a little later in New England.

Then came the gold rush of 1849, and again speed was needed. Clippers took prospectors from New York and Boston to California by way of Cape Horn. And, finally, there was a gold rush in Australia in 1851, and the British ordered clippers for use in the Australian trade.

Everything about the clipper was made for speed. It had a long, slender hull with a long, sharp bow that clipped through the waves. Its three slanted masts carried a cloud of sail, including topgallant and royal sails, and sometimes skysails and moonrakers to capture the power of the winds that wander over the seas.

The sharpest and fastest of the clippers was the Lightning, *which was built in America to British order for the Australian trade.*

Clippers set all sorts of records. The *Sovereign of the Seas* sailed from New York to San Francisco in 103 days, and back in eighty-two. She once made 5,200 miles in three weeks, and she could do 360 miles a day when the wind was right. The *Flying Cloud* did 374 miles a day. The *Flying Fish* made San Francisco in a hundred days, and the *Ino* made New York from Singapore in eighty-six.

Speed like that took seamen as well as ships. Yankee captains drove their crews hard, but they knew the ways of sea, wind, and sail.

When clippers were first built, steamships were slow and clumsy. But by 1850, steamers were crossing from New York to Liverpool in less than eleven days. This was better than the clipper *Lightning*'s record of thirteen days, nineteen and a half hours.

Although clippers were built until the late 1860's, steam now ruled the waves. The clippers vanished. They left only the memory of their speed and beauty, their long sweeping hulls and clouds of sail, and the music of their names—*Flying Cloud, Zephyr, Witch of the Waves, Cutty Sark*— to haunt the seas forever.

(Next page) This painting of the clipper Zephyr *was made by William Bygrave and shows the ship as she appeared in Messina Harbor, Sicily, in 1860.*▶

THE WAY THEY GO TO CALIFORNIA.

Shipowners used cards like these to advertise clipper sailings to California. The cartoon (above) makes fun of the Gold Rush. Note the airship and rocket.

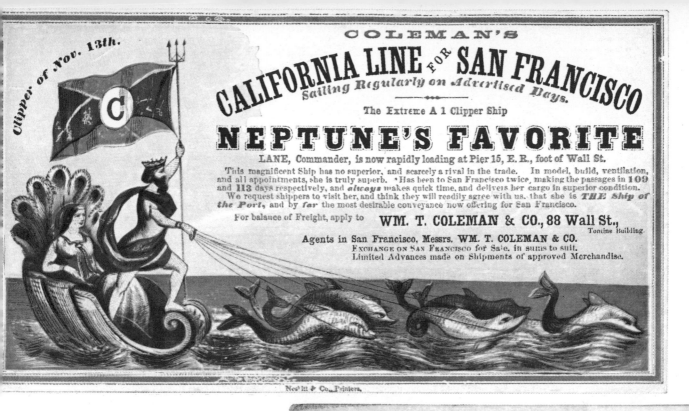

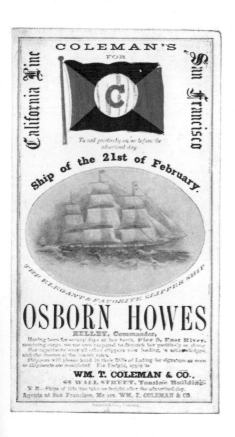

Sir William Drummond Stewart

The First Dude Ranch Trip

In May, 1843, a strange column of riders, pack mules, and covered wagons headed west across the Missouri plains. In the wagons were tents, India-rubber boats, costly wines, potted meats, jams, and other expensive foods and gear. About forty young American sportsmen—including lawyers, doctors, businessmen and scientists—rode at the head of the column. They were going for a summer of fun and hunting in the greatest wilds of all, the Rocky Mountains.

Sir William Drummond Stewart, a Scottish nobleman, was the organizer and leader of the "Sporting Expedition to the West." He had spent six years in the Rockies, and was leading a party of paying guests to his favorite lake in the Wind River Mountains.

On the way west the guides took the dudes buffalo hunting. When they arrived at the lake in the mountains, a large party of trappers and Indians from Black's Fork came to join them, and there were feasts of buffalo meat and elk steaks.

The dudes traded their supplies for furs brought by the trappers, and kept the Indian women busy sewing mountain clothes for them. Fishing in the lake was good. Hunting in the mountains was even better, but the dudes left such things as rat-tlesnakes and grizzly bears to the guides.

For two weeks at what is now called Frémont Lake, the dudes had nothing to do but enjoy themselves. Besides hunting and fishing, they went exploring and held horse races with the Indians. Then they started back. It was the first time the Rockies were used as a "dude ranch" playland.

When the Snake Indians came to trade, they held a parade in honor of Sir William.

A scene near the Platte River. Sir William, center, is riding the white horse.

The Hard-Luck Frigate

When Hurricane Connie raced up the East Coast in August, 1955, an odd-looking ship slowly moved up Chesapeake Bay just ahead of the storm. The oldest American fighting ship, the U. S. frigate *Constellation*, with her masts gone and her hull resting in a floating dry dock, was being towed by a tug. Unless she could reach Baltimore before the hurricane struck, she was doomed. Even on her last voyage, the *Constellation* had to fight for her life.

The frigate reached port in time, but

the big celebration which had been planned in her honor had to be postponed because of the storm. That was the way things always worked out with the *Constellation*. She was a hard-luck ship.

A century and a half earlier, during the three years it took to build her, everything went wrong. Supplies of live oak and cordage were somehow lost before they reached the Baltimore shipyard where she was being built. Then all work on her was stopped for a time, because Congress felt that she was no longer needed. But finally she was launched, on September 7, 1797.

In an undeclared naval war with France, the *Constellation* fought a battle with the *Insurgente* of the French Navy in 1799. She captured the French ship after a hard fight, but almost lost her prize in a three-day storm that followed. Within a year after this, she won a battle against the French warship *Vengeance*. But by the time the enemy ship struck her colors, the *Constellation* had lost her mainmast. She was so crippled that the enemy ship got away.

Next she was sent with several other American warships to the Mediterranean, to fight the pirates of Tripoli. But the *Constellation* again missed her chance for glory. She was damaged in a storm and had to return home.

The Constellation *was 164 feet long and had twenty-eight guns on her main deck and twelve on her spar deck. One of her narrowest escapes happened in 1833, when a storm in the Mediterranean nearly sank her.*

This tavern sign was no help to the Constellation, *which did not get into the War of 1812.*

She lay rotting in New York for seven years, and was in no condition for battle when the War of 1812 started. The Navy towed her to Norfolk for repairs, and there a British blockade kept her all during the war. She did not get into a single battle.

In 1842, she went to the Far East. But she arrived too late to take part in the Opium War. For many years she served as a training ship, then again was left to rot.

Recently, when the Navy announced plans to break her up, the people of Baltimore raised funds to bring her back to that city and make her a national shrine. And, even on her last voyage, she was almost destroyed by a storm. That was normal, for she was the hard-luck frigate *Constellation,* and hard luck followed her wherever she went.

It Was Fun
To Be a Soldier

The cover of an 1860 songsheet shows Colonel Elmer Ephraim Ellsworth, arms folded, with one of his Zouave cadets. The artist made a mistake in coloring the coats green instead of blue.

At the very beginning of the Civil War, on the night of May 23, 1861, an army of the North left Washington to invade the South. It marched across the Potomac River on Long Bridge, making for Alexandria, Virginia, a Confederate town just a few miles down the river.

At the head of the army marched the famous First New York Fire Zouaves. They did not look at all like American soldiers. They wore strange-looking uniforms with baggy red trousers and little blue "monkey" jackets.

A famous volunteer company, New York's Seventh Regiment, parades at Washington Square in 1851.

Keeping perfect step, the men tramped through the moonlit night, line after line of them with their bayonets flashing. Each of them looked forward to the coming battle as the beginning of a great adventure. They had never been in a shooting war before, but they felt that it would be a thrilling experience, filled with bright uniforms and waving banners. They had trained hard and long, and they expected to win a quick victory that would make them national heroes.

None of the men had brighter dreams of glory that night than did their young leader, Colonel Elmer Ephraim Ellsworth. Although only twenty-four years old, he was already well known as a military leader. Even President Lincoln spoke of Ellsworth as a remarkable young man who

(Next page) The First Division, New York State Artillery, forming for a parade at Castle Garden. Among those taking part are the Morris Cadets; Hussars; Lafayette, Montgomery, Washington & Brooklyn Horse Guards; National Guards; Washington Greys; Horse Artillery; and Lancers. ▶

would soon be winning honors for himself on the field of battle.

At dawn, Ellsworth and his men reached Alexandria. He led a squad off on a quick march to take the telegraph office. On the way, he saw a Confederate flag waving from the attic window of a hotel known as the Marshall House. He and some of his men went into the hotel, climbed to the attic, and took in the flag.

As they started downstairs they were met by the owner of the hotel, who had a gun. One of the soldiers leaped at the man, but he was too late. The gun went off. Ellsworth was hit in the chest. By the time he had rolled to the foot of the stairs he was dead. He had not done any of the brave things he had dreamed of. But because he

Uniforms of 1839: The Montgomery, Pa., Hibernia Greens (left) and the Albany, N.Y., Burgess Corps.

was the first Union officer to be killed in the war, he became a national hero.

At the time of his death, Ellsworth was considered the top leader of a special kind of military outfit known as the "volunteer militia company." From earliest Colonial days to the time of the Civil War there were two different types of military units in America. One was the standing militia, and the other was the kind Ellsworth had led—the volunteer militia company.

The standing milita was made up of civilians who could be called upon to fight whenever they were needed. The farmers who dropped their plows to fight the British at Lexington and Concord at the beginning of the Revolutionary War were militiamen of this type.

(Below) A lithograph showing a dress parade of officers and men at Camp Onondaga, New York.

A member of the National Lancers, Boston.

Collection of Mrs. John Nicholas Brown

Collection of Mrs. John Nicholas Brown

The artist of this 1830 print was making fun of the standing militia of his day.

But the trouble was that the men of the standing militia were not very good soldiers. They did very little drilling. Their officers were poor. Very few of them had uniforms. When they did have to fight a battle, they would hurry back to their farms as soon as the fighting was over. The standing militia did so poorly in battle that many young men became disgusted with it. These young men wanted to be good soldiers, so they formed volunteer companies of their own.

Probably the first volunteer company in America was the Honorable Artillery Company, formed in Boston in 1638. By 1750, there were volunteer units of this kind in every Colonial city. Smart companies like the New Jersey Blues, Haslet's Delaware Battalion, and Smallwood's

Marylanders were among the best military units to fight the British during the early part of the Revolutionary War. They won high praise from General George Washington.

Between 1840 and 1850, so many volunteer companies were formed in the New England states that the standing militia was no longer needed. All the soldiers who fought in the war with Mexico belonged to volunteer companies, for by that time there were enough of them to create a whole army.

The volunteer units were much better than the old standing militia. The volunteers thought it was fun to be a soldier. Each outfit had a special uniform, the fancier the better, and each man paid for his uniform out of his own pocket. Rifles

The Boston Fusiliers looked like British redcoats. They were organized July 4, 1787.

and other weapons were often borrowed from state governments. They drilled at least once a week, and held target practice, and went on long marches—all at their own expense. They marched in parades whenever they could, and held drill contests with other companies.

Every large city had a number of units. In Boston, for example, there were the Rifle Rangers, who were Republicans; the Winslow Blues, who were Democrats; the Montgomery Guards, who were Irishmen; the Highland Guards, who were Scotsmen; and others.

Most volunteer companies were social clubs as well, and young men found them quite expensive. For one thing, beautiful uniforms were costly. They had to borrow or hire their horses. But the volunteer units had a fine company spirit. Their members were willing to go anywhere, at their own expense, to serve their country.

Elmer Ephraim Ellsworth thought these companies should be even better than they were. He had read all the important military books by the time he was twenty-one, and had some ideas of his own about how volunteer companies could be improved.

From his French fencing master he had heard about a famous fighting outfit of the French Army called the Zouaves. Ellsworth learned French so that he could read French books about the Zouave system of training soldiers. Then he formed a Zouave volunteer company in Chicago. He drilled them for four or five hours, three times a week, until they had mastered some 500 fancy-drill movements.

In September of 1859, he marched them in a drill contest for the "national championship" at a fair in Chicago, and won easily. When other volunteer companies in the South and East heard that Ellsworth's Zouaves claimed the national championship, they laughed. Ellsworth said he would give up the champion colors to any company in the United States or Canada that could win them from his outfit in a fair contest.

He took the Zouaves on a tour through the East in the summer of 1860 to defend the championship. Huge crowds turned out in all the cities they visited, and no one who saw them doubted that they were the champions.

One writer had this to say about them: "Washington was enlivened . . . by a visit from the 'Chicago Zouaves,' a volunteer organization . . . trained . . . in the novel drill based on the quick movements of the Moors. . . . They drilled as light infantry, and moved like electric clocks."

Returning to Chicago, the Zouaves were greeted with fireworks and a torchlight parade, and were treated like conquering heroes. Then Ellsworth resigned and the company broke up.

When President Lincoln called for 75,000 troops on April 15, 1861, Ellsworth formed another company of Zouaves from the firemen of New York City. He and ten officers from his original Zouaves drilled the firemen day after day. On May 7, with President Lincoln there to watch them, they were taken into the United States Army in Washington.

During the Civil War, bright posters like the one at right were used to get men to join volunteer militia companies. (Left) The members of the Putnam Phalanx of Hartford, Connecticut, posed stiffly for this souvenir lithograph.

SPRAGUE
LIGHT CAVALRY!

NOW IS THE TIME TO JOIN THE BEST CORPS IN THE FIELD!

This New and Splendid Regiment is being organized at PLATTSBURGH, N. Y., under the immediate supervision of

Adj't Gen. Sprague,

OF THIS STATE, WHOSE NAME THE REGIMENT BEARS.

☞ Highest Bounties paid Promptly.

☞ The Colonel has carefully inspected the Barracks, and pronounces them the finest and most comfortable in the State. Neat Rooms, well warmed, properly lighted, and good clean beds, furnished to all Recruits immediately on their arrival.

Men allowed to furnish their own Horses

IF IN GOOD CONDITION AND FITTED FOR SERVICE.

☞ ALL RECRUITS UNIFORMED IMMEDIATELY ON ARRIVAL AT CAMP. ☜

The renowned and popular CAPTAIN LOT CHAMBERLAIN, the leading mover of this organization, has the Contract for subsisting the same. The simple fact of his having subsisted Three Regiments, prior to this, is sufficient assurance that the men will be well fed and properly cared for.

SPENCER H. OLMSTED, Col. Commanding.

Clarry & Reilley, Printers & Engravers, 12 & 14 Spruce-st. N. Y.

Levi Berman Collection

Collection of Mrs. John Nicholas Brown

Two short weeks later, they made their night march over Long Bridge to Alexandria, where Ellsworth was shot. His Zouaves continued fighting throughout the Civil War, but they soon changed their fancy clothing for uniforms that were more practical.

The Civil War years were years of death and destruction and misery. By the time they were over, few men thought it was fun to be a soldier. The great days of the volunteer companies had come to an end.

131

Generals of the Union

One of President Lincoln's problems during the Civil War was finding generals who could win battles. The trouble started right at the beginning, when Robert E. Lee was offered the field command of the Union armies. But he turned it down and joined the Confederates.

General Irvin McDowell commanded the Union forces that were beaten in the first battle of Bull Run. Lincoln put General George B. McClellan in his place.

Loan to the Smithsonian Institution by Margaret Garber Blue

McClellan was a good soldier, but he moved too slowly. He took all summer and fall to get his army into shape. By then it was too late to fight before winter set in. The following spring, against Lincoln's wishes, he started a wide swing through Virginia, and was defeated in the Seven Days' Battle.

Lincoln tried General John Pope next. Pope took a beating at the second battle of Bull Run and did not last long. By this time Lincoln had just about run out of generals, and he decided to give McClellan another chance. McClellan stopped Lee at Antietam, but failed to follow him back into Virginia.

Ambrose E. Burnside was then given command of the Army of the Potomac. After his defeat at Fredericksburg, Lincoln replaced him with Joseph Hooker. That did not work out too well, so George G. Meade was given the command. A few days later, Meade stopped the enemy at Gettysburg.

In the west, General Ulysses S. Grant had been winning victories, too. Lincoln made him top general and brought him east to fight against Lee in Virginia.

From then on, Lincoln's trouble with generals was over. Grant, with the aid of Sheridan and Sherman, slowly crushed the South and ended the war.

"Grant and His Generals," painted by Ole Peter Hansen Balling. Left to right: Generals Thomas Devin, George A. Custer, Judson Kilpatrick, W. H. Emory, Philip Sheridan, James B. McPherson, George Crook, Wesley Merritt, George H. Thomas, G. K. Warren, George Gordon Meade, John G. Parke, William T. Sherman, John A. Logan, Ulysses S. Grant, Ambrose E. Burnside, Joseph Hooker, Winfield S. Hancock, John A. Rawlins, E. O. C. Ord, Francis P. Blair, Jr., Alfred H. Terry, Henry W. Slocum, Jefferson Davis (who had the same name as the Confederate president), Oliver O. Howard, John M. Schofield, Joseph A. Mower.

133

Generals of the Confederacy

"Summer" is the title of the above painting of Confederate generals, as they appeared in 1863. The artist, Charles Hoffbauer, finished the canvas in 1920.

From left to right the generals are: John Bell Hood (standing); Wade Hampton (mounted); Richard S. Ewell (foot on stump); John Brown Gordon (arms folded); Thomas J. "Stonewall" Jackson (mounted); Fitzhugh Lee (pointing); Ambrose P. Hill (with sword); Robert E. Lee (on white horse); James Longstreet

(with field glasses); Joseph E. Johnston (mounted); Pierre G. T. Beauregard (holding map); and James E. B. "Jeb" Stuart (beside his horse).

During most of the Civil War, Robert E. Lee was commander of the Army of Northern Virginia. On February 6, 1865, he was appointed commander-in-chief of the Armies of the Confederacy, a position he held until the war ended less than nine weeks later.

Next to Lee, Jackson was the greatest and most loved general of the South. He was given the nickname of "Stonewall" after the first battle of Bull Run, because he and his brigade stood "like a stone wall." He was accidentally shot by his own men at the battle of Chancellorsville, and died about a week later.

Generals Stuart and Hill were also killed during the war. Young "Jeb" Stuart was one of Lee's most trusted officers.

135

The Battle of the Ironclads

Late one afternoon, about a year after the start of the Civil War, a strange warship came sailing into Hampton Roads, Virginia. She was the *Monitor*, the North's first ironclad warship, and she looked like a cheesebox on a raft. Her task was to keep the Confederate ironclad *Merrimac* from destroying a Yankee fleet of wooden frigates.

The famous battle between the two ironclads took place the following day, March 9, 1862. The *Monitor* was the faster of the two ships. Only 172 feet long, she was about half the length of the *Merrimac*. The gun turret on her deck could be turned to aim her guns in any direction— but she had only two guns.

The *Merrimac* had ten guns. Her crew of 300 was more than five times as large as the crew of the little *Monitor*. And yet, in spite of the great differences in size and fire power, the two ships fought for four hours in the most important naval battle of the Civil War.

An artist's impression of the world's first battle between ironclads. Like a "cheesebox on a raft" the Monitor *of the North faced the Confederate ship* Merrimac *at Hampton Roads, Virginia. Although the artist showed many ships at the scene of the battle, the wooden frigate* Minnesota *(right) was actually the only other ship present.*

Second in command of the *Monitor* was Lieutenant S. Dana Greene. He was twenty-two years old and had been out of Annapolis only three years, but when the captain was blinded by gunpowder, he took command of the ship. In a letter to his family a few days later, he gave a full account of the battle.

He began his story with the two-day voyage from New York. The *Monitor* was towed by a paddle steamer and hit rough seas on her first day out. So much water came down the smokestacks that the engine room filled with gas. The men below were overcome and had to be carried up and revived in fresh air.

With the steam pumps dead, the small craft began taking on water rapidly. Lieutenant Greene could not get the hand pump to work. Bailing was almost useless. Luckily, the wind was offshore, and the steamer was able to tow the *Monitor* into smooth water closer to land.

Once the steering wheel jammed. Later,

Lithograph by Henry Bill, 1862

Afloat, the Merrimac *was said to look like a turtle with a smokestack on top.*

the towing hawser broke. But on March 8 she finally passed Cape Henry. And then the crew heard the booming of cannon from the direction of Fort Monroe.

A pilot boat came alongside with the news that the *Merrimac* had already struck at the Yankee frigates. The *Cumberland* had been sunk. The *Congress* was on fire and had surrendered. And, as the *Monitor* approached Hampton Roads, Lieutenant Greene could see the smoke and flames that rose from the *Congress*. But the *Merrimac* was nowhere in sight.

That evening the *Monitor* was ordered to protect the *Minnesota*, which had run aground near Newport News during the battle. The ironclad anchored close to the helpless frigate, and Lieutenant Greene and the captain stayed on deck through the night.

The next morning they saw the *Merrimac* riding at anchor under the Confederate guns at Sewell's Point. At eight o'clock she got under way, making directly for the *Minnesota*.

The *Monitor* was cleared for action. Her men were at their stations, her guns loaded and ready. Soon the command came from

Captain Worden: "Commence firing!" Lieutenant Greene raised the port, ran out the gun, and fired the first shot. The battle was on.

"We loaded and fired as fast as we could—I pointed and fired the guns myself," Greene wrote.

Five times during the battle the two vessels touched each other. Once the *Merrimac* tried to ram the Yankees with her iron prow, but could do no damage. Then around 11:30 A.M. a shot struck the *Monitor's* pilothouse. Captain Worden was blinded, and turned over his command to the young lieutenant.

Greene soon found his ship between the *Minnesota* and the *Merrimac*. Twice the *Monitor* was accidentally hit by shots from the *Minnesota*. But before long the *Merrimac* retreated toward the Confederate guns on Sewell's Point.

"The fight was over now, and we were victorious," wrote Greene. "My men and myself were perfectly black with smoke and powder. . . . As we ran alongside the *Minnesota*, Secretary Fox [Gustavus V. Fox, Assistant Secretary of the Navy] hailed us, and told us we had fought the

Starting at the bow, this cutaway view of the Monitor *shows the anchor housing, pilothouse above decks, crew's quarters, turret, boilers and engines, protected screw and rudder.*

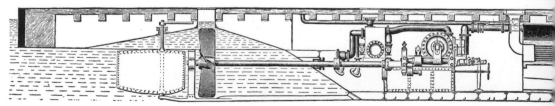

138

From Battles and Leaders of the Civil War

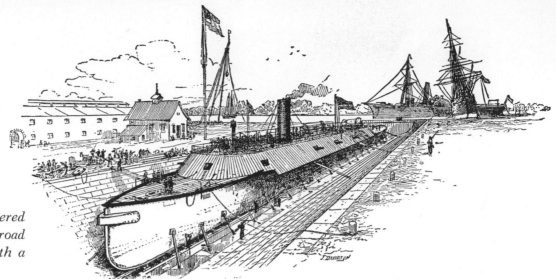

The Merrimac *was covered with four inches of railroad iron, and equipped with a cast-iron ram.*

greatest naval battle on record, and behaved as gallantly as men could."

About the damage suffered by the *Monitor*, he wrote, "The deepest indentation in our sides is 4 inches. Tower 2 inches and deck ½ inch. We were not at all damaged except the pilothouse."

The next day, command of the vessel was taken away from Greene. Secretary Fox felt that he was too young for the job.

"Of course I was a little taken aback at first," Greene said in his letter, "but on second thought I saw it was as it should be." Still, he could not help adding that "between you and me I would have kept the command with all its responsibility and either the *Merrimac* or the *Monitor* should have gone down in our next engagement. But then you know that all young people are vain, conceited & without judgment."

Lieutenant Greene wrote his letter just a few days after the battle, and he expected another fight with the *Merrimac*. But the two vessels never fought again.

Two months later the Confederates pulled out of Norfolk, leaving the *Merrimac* without a base. Too big for the James River, and too unseaworthy to take to sea, she was destroyed by her own crew on May 10. As for the *Monitor*, she was lost in a storm off Cape Hatteras on December 31, 1862.

The fight between the two ships had been a draw, with neither able to cripple the other. But the *Monitor* had saved most of the fleet of frigates, so the North looked upon it as a great victory.

One thing, however, was certain. The battle between the two ironclads proved to the world that the days of wooden fighting ships had come to an end.

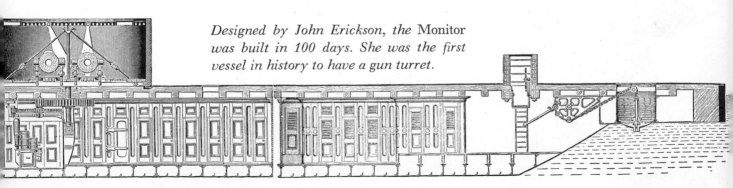

Designed by John Erickson, the Monitor *was built in 100 days. She was the first vessel in history to have a gun turret.*

General Lee's Two Wars

President Jefferson Davis of the Confederacy, a West Point graduate, thought of himself as the best military leader of the South. He was proud and stubborn, and he seldom agreed with Lee.

Brown Brothers

At the beginning of the Civil War, General Robert E. Lee looked like a young man. Although he was fifty-four years old, he had a strong build and he stood erect. His hair and mustache were dark, and he had not yet grown a beard.

By the end of the war, Lee was old, weary, and gray. He had aged more than any other general on either side—probably because he had to fight two wars at the same time.

One of Lee's wars was, of course, fought on the battlefield, against the North. The other war was against Jefferson Davis, President of the Confederacy. Davis was Lee's chief, and the two men did not often

Lee's sword, gloves, and hat, shown against a Confederate flag. Lee was allowed to keep his sword when he surrendered to Grant at Appomattox.

Photograph by Bradley Smith

agree. Lee was loyal to Davis, but there was trouble from the start. Lee wanted to lead an army. Davis kept him at a desk for a year. Lee believed in attack. Davis thought his armies should stay in the South and defend the Confederacy.

When Lee was at last given command of an army, he fought his own kind of war. In less than three months he drove out the enemy and invaded the North. Even then, Davis kept a large number of soldiers on guard duty in Virginia. So it happened that one-fourth of Pickett's crack troops were guarding a supply depot near Virginia during the important battle of Gettysburg.

No Civil War general on either side aged more than did General Lee. At left, Lee was a strong and young-looking man just before the war. At right, as he looked after the war—tired and gray.

Lee lost the battle. Could he have won with the extra men? No one knows. But no one doubts that fighting two wars at the same time left Lee an old man.

Collection of items of Jefferson Davis, including slippers, pocket compass, and pen case. Davis was captured after the war, but was later released.

Death on the Dark River

Harper's Weekly, *May 20, 1865*

The steamboat Sultana *in flames on the Mississippi, as shown in an old engraving.*

It was April of 1865, and flood waters were
overflowing the banks of the Mississippi.
But no one gave much attention to the
tricks of the river, for the Civil War had
ended at last, and there was peace in the
land. There was peace—but a bitterness,
a sadness, a great weariness hung heavily
over the men who had fought. They were
sick of war and wanted to go home.

At Vicksburg, thousands of Union soldiers were gathered, waiting to be sent
north. They were all anxious to get
started, but the most anxious were those
who had just been freed from southern
prison camps. Pale and weak, too thin for
their faded blue uniforms, they could
think only of home. They badly needed
rest and care and good food, and their
families about them.

And so, when the steamboat *Sultana*
made a landing at Vicksburg, the soldiers
rushed to get aboard. As they tramped up
the gangplank, they laughed and sang and
joked and shouted. The war was over,
and they were going home.

They jammed the hurricane deck, the
texas deck, the lower deck, the boiler deck.

They crowded into the hull, the cabins,
even the pilothouse. And still they came,
until the steamer could hold no more.
There were about 2,300 persons on a boat
meant to carry 376.

Only the *Sultana*'s captain, J. C. Mason,
was worried. He had had trouble with the
boilers, and the river's current was un-
usually strong. But the boat eased away
from the wharf and went puffing up-
stream, and forty-eight hours later put in
at Memphis.

A number of soldiers went ashore to see
the sights, and some of them did not get
back by sailing time. They must have
cursed their luck when they found that
the boat had left without them.

Meanwhile, *the Sultana* was pushing on
through the night, her big paddle wheels
beating against the strong current. Mid-
night passed, and one o'clock. Around two
in the morning she swung around a bend
of the dark river—and then it happened.

The boilers exploded with a tremendous
crash, and flames roared up into the dark
sky. Hundreds of soldiers were blown into
the river. Red-hot coals, twisted machin-
ery, bits and pieces of wood, furniture,
railings, deck beams flew through the air.
The boat caught fire, and the soldiers still

aboard had to leap into the icy-cold water or be burned alive.

Many of the men could not swim. And even those who could swim were too weak from months of prison to fight the water. Shouting and screaming, they thrashed about, reaching for any bit of wreckage that might keep them afloat.

"The ship is sinking!" someone cried. A hundred voices repeated, "The ship is sinking! The ship is sinking!" And, with a great hissing noise, the *Sultana* went down to the bottom of the Mississippi.

In the first light of dawn, rescue ships came steaming up from Memphis. Although they picked up hundreds of survivors, they were too late. About 1,700 men were dead in one of the worst steamboat accidents in history.

There was peace in the land. The fighting was ended. The rifles and the cannon were silent. But the dead of the *Sultana* had been killed by war, just as surely as if they had been shot down in battle.

Photograph by Carl Fischer

It Happens Every Four Years

Every four years a strange sort of madness seems to come over Americans. The country blossoms out with posters, banners, and signs. There are parades and big meetings. Speeches and the sound of cheering crowds fill the air. A visiting foreigner might think that Americans had gone a little crazy. But it is just another Presidential year, when the voters decide who will be the next President of the United States.

Before there can be an election, each political party must choose its candidate for President. And so each party holds a convention—a meeting of delegates representing party members of every state. They get together in a brightly decorated hall, where they listen to speeches, parade around with banners, and shout for their favorite candidates.

At the same time, much of the serious

New York's Tammany Hall, decorated for the 1868 Democratic convention which nominated Horatio Seymour. He lost to Ulysses S. Grant.

Whig campaign ribbon of 1844. Ribbons had already been used by the thousands in the 1840 campaign.

Delegates to the Democratic convention of 1900 wore ribbons with patriotic symbols. Their candidate, William Jennings Bryan, lost the election.

business of the convention is done by committees meeting in small rooms. At last the list of candidates is narrowed down to a few men, and the delegates take a vote. Then the winning candidates for President and Vice-President are brought into the hall to be introduced, and to make speeches accepting their nomination.

Political conventions have long been the American way of nominating candidates for President. And yet the Constitution says nothing about conventions. In fact, it says nothing on how candidates are to be nominated.

In the early days of the United States, there were no political conventions. The congressmen of each party held meetings to nominate their candidates. But as the country grew, this system became more and more unpopular.

145

Then, around 1830, a small political party, called the Anti-Mason Party, was formed. Its members believed that too many Masons were being elected to high offices in the government. The new party wanted to nominate its own candidate for President. But it could not do so in the usual way, for none of its members were in Congress.

The Anti-Masons decided to hold a political convention. They met in 1831 and nominated William Wirt as their candidate, to run against Andrew Jackson and Henry Clay, who were both Masons. This was the first time in American history that a political convention was held to nominate a candidate. Members of the other parties thought it was a good idea, and by 1840 they were all holding conventions. Candidates have been nominated in this way ever since.

At first, the winning candidates often had to be told of their nomination by mail. The postage rate then was ten cents for each letter. Stamps had not been used for very long, and people often forgot to put them on. That meant that the person receiving the letter had to pay a dime for postage. Mail service was not very good, and strange things were bound to happen once in a while.

When Zachary Taylor was nominated, he lived in Louisiana. He had been receiving many letters from supporters and cranks, and he had to pay for most of them himself. One day he grew tired of it and refused to accept a large bundle of letters. They were sent to Washington as unclaimed mail. Later, Taylor changed his mind, paid the postage, and had the letters sent back to him. In the bundle was the official letter telling of his nomination. Taylor read it almost a month after the convention was over.

None of the early candidates made campaign speeches. They felt that it would not be dignified for them to work for their own election. Thomas Jefferson did write letters, however, trying to get others to fight for his election while he remained quietly at home.

William Henry Harrison seems to have been the first candidate to make speeches. In the campaign of 1836, he toured several states and spoke a number of times. Four years later he was at it again. This was the famous campaign in which Harrison's name was linked with log cabins, hard cider, and coonskin caps. His party wanted to show that he was on the side of the poor and the people who lived in the western part of the country. Harrison was called "Old Tippecanoe," to remind the voters that he was the hero who had fought the Indians at Tippecanoe Creek.

It turned out to be one of the wildest campaigns in American history. Mass meetings were held in public parks, and newspapers reported that the crowds gathered "by the acre." There were grand parades with bands and drum and bugle corps, and in each one there was a log cabin on wheels. Free sandwiches were passed out at big barbecues.

At night there were more parades. The marchers carried flaming torches and sang as they stepped along. So many campaign songs were written for Harrison and his party that people lost count of them. One songbook alone contained a hundred of these songs.

Men who wanted Harrison for President shouted slogans as if they were war

This Republican poster of 1896 compares the good times under the Republicans with the bad times under the Democrats. McKinley wanted high tariffs on goods imported from foreign countries.

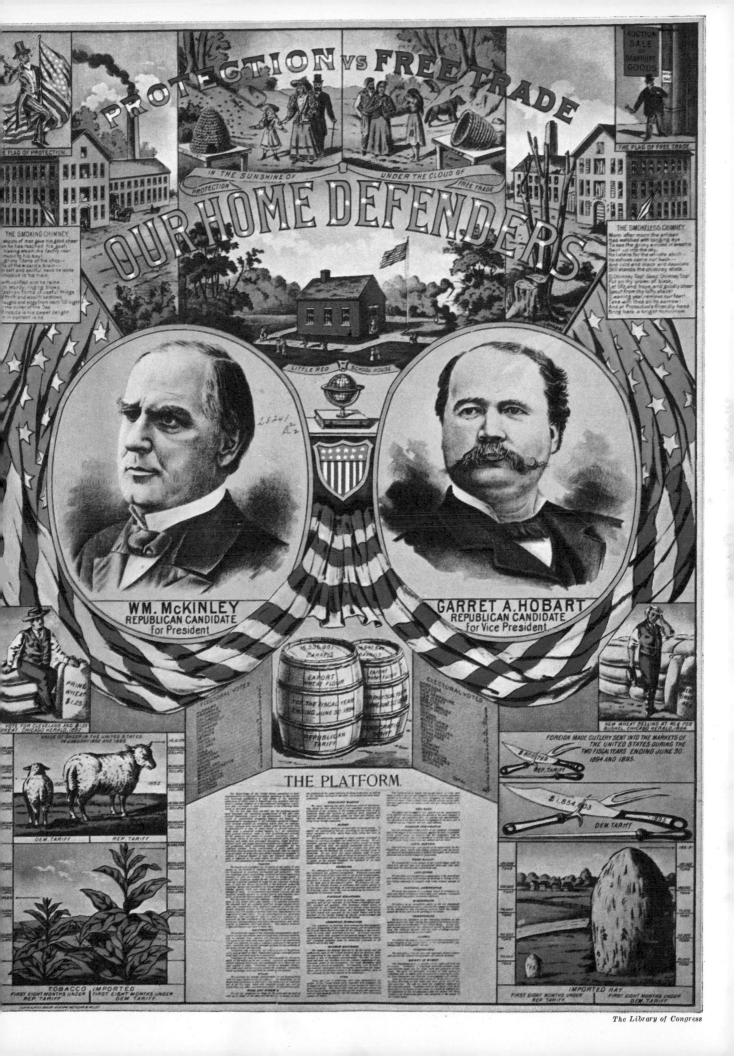

Presidential campaign buttons did not come into wide use until after the Civil War. Since then they have been used by the millions in one campaign after another.

This poster by the famous Currier & Ives failed to help McClellan, who lost the election to Lincoln.

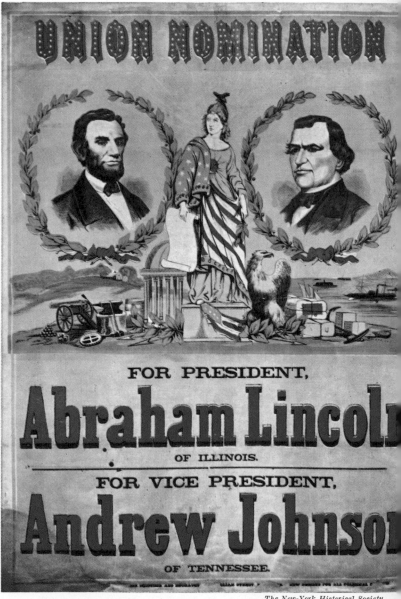

Grover Cleveland was linked with the White House in this ribbon of the campaign of 1892.

When Lincoln ran for his second term in 1864, his chances were improved by northern victories in the Civil War. Lincoln made no campaign speeches.

This 1904 Teddy Roosevelt poster was meant to appeal to farmers.

A political handkerchief of the "Log Cabin and Hard Cider" campaign of the Whigs in 1840. Their slogan, "Tippecanoe and Tyler, Too!" is one of the most famous ever used in American politics.

cries. John Tyler was the candidate for Vice-President, and the most popular of the slogans was "Tippecanoe and Tyler, Too!" Harrison was running against Martin Van Buren, who was mentioned in such slogans as: "Farewell, dear Van, you're not our man!" and "With Tip and Tyler we'll burst Van's biler!" And for the first time thousands of badges, ribbons, and banners were used in a political campaign to help stir up voters.

Harrison won the election. But most people felt that it was not proper for a candidate to make speeches, and it was not tried again for many years. Abraham Lincoln, for example, made no campaign speeches in 1860 or 1864. But Benjamin Harrison in 1888, and William McKinley, in 1896, made speeches from their front porches to visiting delegates. From that time on, all candidates have taken an active part in their own campaigns.

With the invention of radio, candidates were able to reach a greater number of voters than ever before. The first broadcast of a convention came in 1924. Eight years later, Franklin D. Roosevelt started something new when he appeared on the convention floor after his nomination and made an acceptance speech. Other candidates since then have followed his example. And, beginning in 1952, television has brought the excitement of political conventions into the homes of millions of Americans.

Some historians believe that there is one danger in political conventions. The people who have the most to say about running the conventions are professional politicians. These men are the leaders of the political parties, and their business is politics. Sometimes they are more interested in the problems of the party than in the problems of the government.

But political conventions and cam-

paigns seem to be here to stay. Voters find them fun, but they also take them seriously. As long as they do, the convention and campaign system will work, and work pretty well. For, in a democracy, it is the voters who have the final say.

The Lost Bet *is the title of this painting by Joseph Klir. The scene is Chicago's West 12th Street. The man acting as horse is a Republican who made the mistake of betting that his candidate, Benjamin Harrison, would win the election in 1892. The driver is the winner. He bet on Grover Cleveland.*

The Overland Stage

"Here comes the stage!" At this shout, everyone in the little town of Tipton, Missouri, rushed out into the street. A few minutes later a dusty stagecoach came to a stop before the cheering crowd.

The date was October 9, 1858, and the first Overland Mail stage had finished its long run from San Francisco in twenty-three days and four hours. That was the beginning of regular, twice-a-week service between California and Tipton, end of the railroad line from the East.

For a year, John Butterfield and his partners had been at work, organizing the big cross-country stage line. Roads, bridges, and ferries had to be built. Stations had to be put up every twenty miles along the 2,800-mile route, and water wells had to be dug. The line needed 1,800 horses and mules, 250 coaches, and about 1,000 employees to keep the stages rolling with passengers and mail.

Now, after almost a million dollars had been spent, the line was open for business. Passengers could board a train in New York and travel by rail to Tipton. From there the Overland Stage would carry them south and west through El Paso, Texas, and Tucson, Arizona, to Los Angeles and San Francisco.

There was always danger of an attack by Indians when the Overland Stage traveled between Missouri and California—but such an attack happened only once. Frederic Remington painted this scene.

From Frederic Remington *by Harold McCracken; courtesy J. B. Lippincott Company*

152

The stagecoach journey took about twenty-five days and cost $200. Passengers were allowed forty pounds of luggage—the same as that allowed by airlines today. The coaches rolled night and day, stopping at the stations to change horses and drivers, and to let the passengers get something to eat. The trip was not easy. As one traveler described it, "To feel oneself bouncing—now on the hard seat, now against the roof . . . was no joke."

The coaches did not carry shipments of gold or silver, and so they were never held up by bandits. And only once was there an attack by Indians. Regular mail service continued without a break until the Civil War. Then the line went by a more direct route through South Pass and Salt Lake City. The Overland Stage was sold to Wells, Fargo in 1866, but began to lose its importance when the Union Pacific Railroad was completed three years later.

General George Armstrong Custer

The Man Who Killed Custer*

The Battle of the Little Big Horn, which was fought on June 25, 1876, was not a big battle, nor was it a very important one. But it has never been forgotten. At Little Big Horn the Indians wiped out General George Armstrong Custer and his troops, and the news shocked the nation.

Custer had divided his men into four

groups, one of them under a major named Reno, and sent them off in different directions. There was an Indian camp somewhere ahead, but he did not know exactly where it was. He hoped to find it and attack from several directions at once.

Major Reno's men were attacked by the Indians and driven back with heavy losses. But Custer knew nothing of this. He was leading about 225 men along the brown bluffs near the river when he was suddenly surprised by a large force of Indians. They came at him from all sides, and not one soldier escaped in the slaughter that followed.

Only the Indians who took part in the battle knew the true story of what happened that day. To get the story, writer Stanley Vestal visited the Cheyenne River Sioux Reservation in 1932, and questioned old Chief White Bull.

At the time of the battle, Chief White Bull was twenty-six years old. He told how he and about a thousand braves had driven Major Reno's troops across the river. Then they heard that more soldiers, Custer's men, were coming from the east, and the braves rushed to meet them.

Chief White Bull did not speak of the number of soldiers he killed that day. The greatest honor for an Indian came from a "coup"—touching or hitting a living man. White Bull told how he hit one soldier on the ground, dragged another from his horse, and rode down two others. Then his horse was shot from under him, but by that time only a few soldiers were left.

Chief White Bull said, "I charged in. A tall, well-built soldier with yellow hair and mustache saw me coming and tried to bluff me. . . . But when I rushed him, he threw his rifle at me without shooting. I dodged it. We grabbed each other and wrestled there in the dust and smoke. . . . This soldier was very strong and brave. He

* Adapted from The Man Who Killed Custer, by Stanley Vestal. © 1957 by the University of Oklahoma Pre

Chief White Bull's own drawing of his fight with Custer.

tried to wrench my rifle from me. I lashed him across the face with my quirt, striking the coup. He let go, then grabbed my gun with both hands until I struck him again.

"But the tall soldier fought hard. He was desperate. He hit me with his fists on the jaw and shoulders, then grabbed my long braids with both hands, pulled my face close and tried to bite my nose off. . . . I thought that soldier would kill me. . . .

"Finally I broke free. He drew his pistol. I wrenched it out of his hand and struck him with it three or four times on the head, knocked him over, shot him in the head, and fired at his heart. . . ."

Later, White Bull said, he learned that the man he had killed was Custer. Stanley Vestal kept White Bull's secret, fearing that some hothead might try to harm the old man. But now White Bull is dead, and his story can be told.

Chief White Bull in his old age.

156

The Old Country Store

PET OF THE HOUSEHOLD.

Farm wives and children liked to collect colored advertising cards like this one, which country merchants handed out to their customers.

The old country store was more than a store. It was an old men's clubhouse, a meeting place for friends and neighbors, a bank, and a safe place where Pa could leave the children when he went to see the blacksmith about shoes for his horses. It was also a United States Post Office, fourth class.

Somewhere in the store was a door, a wall, or a post that served as a bulletin board. On it were notices about horse thieves, church socials, elections, turkey shoots, farm auctions, school doings, and other neighborhood affairs.

There was always a hitch rack or a shed shelter nearby for the free parking of horses, wagons, and bobsleds. The windows were not much to look at. They were usually filled with

What life was like about fifty years ago in the old country store.

The Thrill That Comes Once in a Lifetime BY H. T. WEBSTER

157

notions, spectacles, gilt jewelry and combs, just stored there in a jumble. It did not matter, for few people looked in the windows and there was no other store anywhere around.

Out front there were usually some benches along the wall where the old men and the loafers could sit and visit by the hour. They would get out their knives and whittle, or clean their pipes, just to be doing something. And they would talk about politics, crops, the weather, the great comet of 1881, or tell tall tales of farming, fishing, fighting, and hunting.

But come hog-killing time, when a hint of frost and snow was in the air, they would move inside. They would sit around the iron chunk stove, glowing cherry-red from its fire, and the talk would start again. Once in a while, when the storekeeper was not looking, they would help themselves to a cracker from the big, open barrel.

Not that the storekeeper minded. These men were all old customers and friends, and bought their smoking and "eating" tobacco from him.

The storekeeper himself was likely to be one of the most important men in the community. Besides being the postmaster, he was often the clerk of the town and the keeper of the land records. Sometimes, too, he was the justice of the peace. He would perform marriages and act as a judge when some troublemaker was brought in for trial.

A storekeeper usually picked up a great deal of knowledge about a great many things. He could explain puzzling laws, or write a contract of sale for any of his customers who needed one. He could also doctor a horse, and he gave free medical advice to people with sickness in the family. On several shelves of his store were bottles of patent medicines of all kinds.

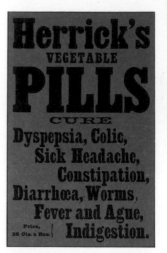

They were sure cures for every human illness ever heard of, and for a few that were not.

The country store sold almost everything, but it sold the most of almost everything just before Christmas. Early in the fall the storekeeper spent hours at his roll-top desk, ordering what he needed for his Christmas trade. The shipment would arrive sometime in November, hauled from the railroad station miles away in a big wagon drawn by horses.

158

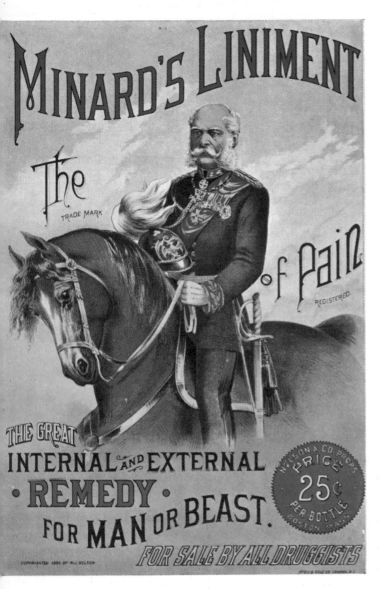

These posters, trade cards, and pamphlets advertised health aids and patent medicines that claimed to cure almost anything. Country stores sold many medicines of this kind to their customers, who did not seem to suffer from them.

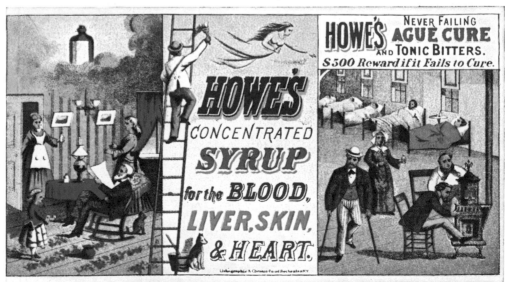

Pictures from the Warshaw Collection of Business Americana

159

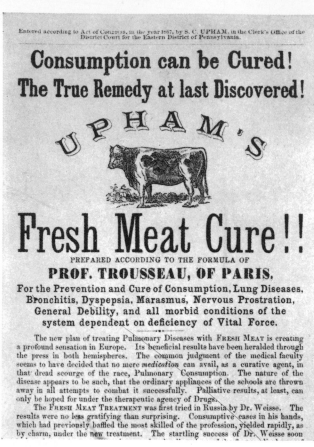

Entered according to Act of Congress, in the year 1867, by S. C. UPHAM, in the Clerk's Office of the District Court for the Eastern District of Pennsylvania.

Consumption can be Cured!
The True Remedy at last Discovered!

UPHAM'S

Fresh Meat Cure!!

PREPARED ACCORDING TO THE FORMULA OF
PROF. TROUSSEAU, OF PARIS,

For the Prevention and Cure of Consumption, Lung Diseases, Bronchitis, Dyspepsia, Marasmus, Nervous Prostration, General Debility, and all morbid conditions of the system dependent on deficiency of Vital Force.

The new plan of treating Pulmonary Diseases with FRESH MEAT is creating a profound sensation in Europe. Its beneficial results have been heralded through the press in both hemispheres. The common judgment of the medical faculty seems to have decided that no more *medication* can avail, as a curative agent, in that dread scourge of the race, Pulmonary Consumption. The nature of the disease appears to be such, that the ordinary appliances of the schools are thrown away in all attempts to combat it successfully. Palliative results, at least, can only be hoped for under the therapeutic agency of Drugs.
The FRESH MEAT TREATMENT was first tried in Russia by Dr. Weisse. The results were no less gratifying than surprising. Consumptive cases in his hands, which had previously baffled the most skilled of the profession, yielded rapidly, as by charm, under the new treatment. The startling success of Dr. Weisse soon

Warshaw Collection

Unloading was quite a chore. There were large wooden packing cases, barrels and bales of all sorts of things. There were boxes of figs, crates of oranges, jute bags of coconuts and English walnuts, wooden pails of stick candy with barber-pole stripes. The weekly paper at the county seat would tell about the big shipment, and every country family would plan a visit to the store to look over the new holiday goods.

The trip from farm to store was usually made on a Saturday. The farmer would hitch up his horse to the farm wagon. He'd put in a few live chickens with their legs tied together, a can of cream, and as much butter as he had on hand. His boys took along the skins of any wild animals they had trapped, and Mother was sure to bring some eggs. The egg money was always hers to use as she liked. The whole family climbed into the wagon, and the

children sat on straw spread on the floor. Then off they went.

The children especially loved to visit the country store. The place was full of strange and exciting smells. The shelves and counters were jammed and crammed with all kinds of things to see. There were even things hanging from hooks on the ceiling—corn poppers, lanterns, pails, and kitchen pots.

The farmer would usually stop at the men's wear counter, piled high with jeans and shirts and shoes. Then he would go to the rear of the store to see the farm tools and heavy hardware. While Mother examined the new dress goods in the ladies' department, the boys hurried back for a look at the hunting knives and the Stevens single-shot .22 caliber rifle.

Meanwhile, the smaller children would have their noses pressed against the glass of the candy case. They stared in wonder at the peppermint sticks, rock candy, horehound drops, lemon drops, and licorice shoestrings, called "likerish" by almost everyone.

After the family had bought all the things they wanted, their purchases were wrapped in brown paper. Sometimes the storekeeper would throw in a red-and-blue striped bag of jellybeans for the children. Then, after the farmer talked a bit with the storekeeper and the men around the stove, he would lead his family outside to the wagon for the trip home. They would visit the country store a number of times during the year, but none of the visits was as much fun as the one at the Christmas season.

The Camera Looks at America

The earliest American photograph still in existence was taken in 1839. It shows the Central High School Building in Philadelphia.

The first photographs were called daguerreotypes. They were named after Louis Daguerre, the French inventor of the camera. This daguerreotype was taken at Niagara Falls.

161

Daguerreotype by D. McDonnell, Buffalo Historical Society

Samuel F. B. Morse, the inventor, brought the first camera to America from Paris. As early as 1850, Americans were taking "news photographs" like the one above of ruins after a fire in Buffalo.

The five daguerreotypes below fit together to form a panorama of San Francisco Harbor. Taken about 1850, they show ships left to rot during the gold rush. The crews had deserted to hunt for gold.

The Smithsonian Institution

In 1854, an unknown cameraman caught the look of an Indian camp in Minneapolis.

This daguerreotype shows the volunteer regiment of Colonel Ellis on parade in San Francisco about 1856. In the background are ships' masts.

Robert Cornelius, a Philadelphia lampmaker, took his own picture in 1839.

A toleware maker with the tools of his trade, photographed in the 1850's.

Woodsawyer's Nooning is the title of this daguerreotype of an old workman and his young apprentice who have stopped work to have lunch.

A clamp was often used to steady the head of the person posing for a photograph.

◄ *These bold firemen had their picture taken in the 1850's.*

This dandy posed in the 1850's for Mathew Brady, a famous photographer of famous people.

This gold miner of the 1850's expected to strike it rich.

166

(Below) Clowning with hoops used in hoop skirts and an empty bottle in front of a store in San Francisco around 1855.

The city marshal of Worcester, Massachusetts, had his picture taken with a prisoner sometime around 1858.

A blacksmith and a Negro boy of Galena, Illinois.

Mother and child
face the camera.

The dog remained still long enough to get in the
picture with his master.

A small boy of the
1850's.

A family group. The man at left is holding a chest of medicines.

Builders for the Carriage Trade

John D. Rockefeller bought this drop-center landau in 1891 for $1,750 (rubber tires $100 extra).

When William Brewster quit his job as head of the famous carriage-building firm of Brewster & Company, in November, 1927, he put an end to a family history of carriage and car building that had lasted more than 100 years. During that time, his grandfather, his father, and he himself had made the name Brewster stand for the very finest in horse carriages.

Every carriage they made was of such quality and beauty that few other carriage makers could hope to equal them. Because so many of their customers were famous Americans, the firm's account books are now kept in The New York Public Library and The New York Historical Society collection.

The period when horse carriages were popular did not last much more than 100 years. Crude carts and farm wagons were all that were built in the American colonies until about 1750. And very few carriages were in use when James, the first of the carriage-making Brewsters, was born in Preston, Connecticut, in 1788.

At the age of fifteen James Brewster became an apprentice to a carriage maker in Northampton, Massachusetts. But the carriage maker was a poor businessman and soon went out of business. With thirty dollars in his pocket, young James headed for New York by coach in 1809. The coach broke down in New Haven, Connecticut. While he was waiting for it to be repaired, James walked about the town and came

This smart two-horse vis-à-vis, with sunshade, was purchased for $1,400 in 1881 by Dr. W. S. Webb.

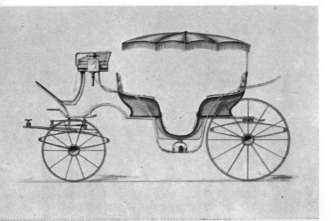

This flashy eight-spring carriage, known as a chariot D'Orsay, was for formal affairs.

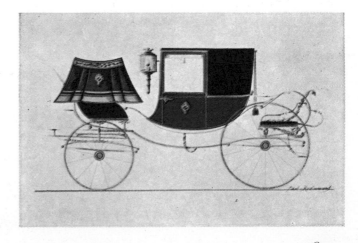

to the carriage shop of John Cook. Cook needed a helper and offered him a job. James took it.

He worked for Cook for about a year, and was able to save $250 out of his salary of a little over five dollars a week. Then he got married, and started a carriage shop of his own. He worked hard, and found many ways of improving the carriages of the time.

Brewster's carriages were the best on the market, and business soon became so good that his shop grew in size. By 1830, he was shipping two-wheel carriages to Mexico, South America, and Cuba. In those countries, carriages were taxed according to the number of wheels they had. The tax on a two-wheeler was half what it was on a carriage with four wheels.

Brewster's business became so good that he opened a branch factory and warehouse in New York in 1827, and later in Bridgeport, Connecticut. These new places were run by his sons, James B. and Henry.

In the 1860's, Central Park was a kind of parade ground for the elegant carriages of the rich. Mr. Brewster, the finest carriage maker in the land, probably would not have approved of this Currier & Ives print. A coachman was not supposed to wear a mustache, and he was expected to keep his elbows close to his body while driving.

170

Cornelius Vanderbilt drove this small mail phaeton in 1872. Two grooms sat in the back seat.

It was Henry, together with two new partners, who took over the business when his father retired in 1856. The name of the firm was then changed to Messrs. Brewster & Company of Broome Street.

The company moved its headquarters from New Haven to New York, where wealthy people were becoming more and more interested in fancy horse carriages. About 20,000 New Yorkers were driving flashy carriages at that time. Society people wanted the very best that was made, and were willing to pay $1,000 to $1,500 for a "close" carriage, or a "close-quarter" coach. They also liked styles known as the caleche, the coupé, and the phaeton, which cost from $350 to $500 each.

This coupé D'Orsay, a less formal version of the chariot D'Orsay, belonged to Pierre Lorillard.

Henry Brewster, who was once called "the best-dressed fat man in America," was proud of his carriages, and wanted to show them in Europe. He wanted to prove to the people of other countries that his coaches were as good as any in the world.

There were a number of reasons why Brewster had such faith in his carriages. Only American carriages had bent wheel rims and spokes made of hickory wood, which had more strength and bounce than any other wood used for wheels. As a result, the wheels were lighter and stronger than those made in other countries. Brewster used elm for hubs. It was tougher and did not split as easily as English oak. His whitewood panels were lighter and cheaper than the mahogany panels of the British and the walnut panels of the French. His carriages had a glass-like polish that other makers could not match. But perhaps his greatest improvement was the use of steel to take the place of the heavy wooden framework.

Brewster's chance to show the world came in 1878, at the French International Exposition. The best carriage builders in the world gathered in Paris for the big fair. There were seventy-two carriages from England and Scotland, including those made by Hooper and Barker, who built the Queen's carriages. French makers showed 222 carriages. Markoff of Russia, builder for the Tsar, arrived with twenty-one carriages. The United States showed thirty-five, and thirteen of these were made by Brewster.

The judges declared Brewster the winner, and gave him the gold medal. The President of France awarded him the Legion of Honor. Americans were proud of their world-champion carriage maker.

Brewster's business became better than ever. From 1881 to 1882, the company took in $435,791. Among its famous customers was John Jacob Astor, who paid $699 for a two-horse cabriolet sleigh, complete with double chimes, pompon, and

Museum of the City of New York

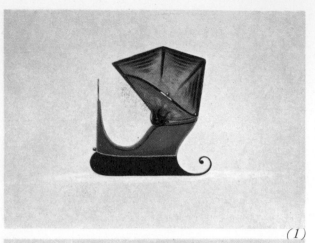

(1)

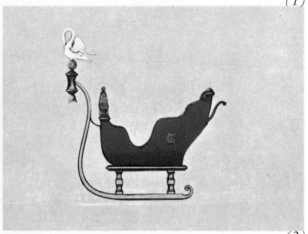

(2)

(3)

(4)

switches. J. Pierpont Morgan bought nearly $1,800 worth of rumble sleighs and a cabriolet in November, 1881. J. R. Roosevelt paid $2,400 for a four-horse drag. William Rockefeller bought a pony cart.

Some society families wanted their carriages painted a certain color, so they could be recognized when driving through the park and the city streets. Brewster made up special colors for them. There was the Vanderbilt maroon, for example, and the Astor blue, and the blue and primrose of the Stevens family.

Young William Brewster joined his father's business in 1883. He worked as an apprentice for four years, then visited all the carriage makers in Europe. After he came back to work, no carriage left the shop without his careful inspection. If he found one flaw in the varnish, he took out his knife and scratched an X across the panel, so that the entire finish had to be done over.

With the coming of the automobile, the carriage trade slowly died. For a time William made car bodies for expensive foreign cars, including the English Rolls-Royce. The Rolls-Royce Company bought his firm in 1925, and he stayed on as an officer for two years. But he did not like the new fast method of making cars, so he left the company.

For over 100 years the Brewsters had made the very finest product in their field, and William Brewster could not be satisfied with anything less.

(1) A tub sleigh of 1878. These were often made in small sizes for children, to be drawn by a pony. (2) The 1880 model cutter of the Portland type was just right for a brisk sleigh ride for two. (3) A push sleigh of 1881. The lady sat inside, pushed along by her gentleman friend on skates. (4) This fancy 1885 German rumble sleigh was driven by a coachman who sat on the rear seat.

The grand saloon of the Bristol, *a luxurious steamer that sailed Long Island Sound.*

The Old Fall River Line

"Heard about the steamboat race? The *Oregon* against the *C. Vanderbilt*—up the Hudson River! From the Battery in New York City to Ossining, then back again! Should be a humdinger!"

In the spring of 1847, all New York was talking about the coming race. And no wonder. The two boats were giant side-wheelers, part of the famous fleet that sailed the Hudson River and Long Island Sound. They were the most modern, most beautiful passenger boats anyone could imagine—and that included the owners. They had spent thousands of dollars to make their boats big, fast, and fancy.

George Law, a steamboat owner, was so proud of his *Oregon* that he offered to race her against any boat that sailed the Sound. Commodore Vanderbilt, whose boat was named after himself, took up the challenge.

New Yorkers could not have asked for a better free show. It looked like an even race. Both boats were new. Both were passenger steamers making regular runs be-

The route of the Fall River Line.

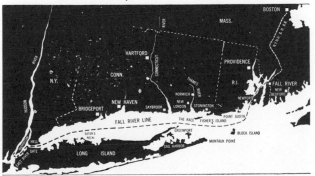

This scene at the New York piers in 1905 is from an old poster. It shows the flagship Priscilla *and two other steamers of the Fall River line. These were the fastest passenger ships in the coastwise trade, making regular runs up Long Island Sound to Fall River, Massachusetts. The* Priscilla, *one of the last ships of the line, was sailing until 1937.*

tween New York and Stonington, Connecticut. The loser was to pay the winner $1,000, but no one cared about the money.

The real prize was the honor of winning.

Getting the boats ready for the race was a big job in itself. They were stripped down. Everything heavy that could be spared was removed. The bottoms of the boats were cleaned in drydock so that they would slip through the water faster, and the engines were tuned up.

The race began at the Battery in New York on a bright, sunny morning in June.

The Mariners Museum, Newport News, Va.

Thousands of people cheered as the *Oregon* and the *C. Vanderbilt* steamed up the Hudson River. Neither boat seemed able to gain on the other. For thirty miles their big paddlewheels thrashed at top speed, but their bows were still even at the turning point at Ossining.

Both boats made a sharp turn at the same moment, and slammed together. It was not a bad accident. The *Oregon's*

wheelhouse was damaged, but she did not slow down. Aboard the *C. Vanderbilt*, the Commodore and his pilot got their signals crossed in the confusion. So many signal bells sounded in the engine room that the puzzled chief engineer stopped the engine dead. Before the boat could start off again, George Law in his *Oregon* had a fine lead.

But the race was not over yet. Trying to save as much weight as possible, Law had

175

TEMPERANCE CONVENTION.

WITH *Banner* and with *Badge* we come,
An *Army* true and strong,
To Fight against the hosts of *Rum*,
And this shall be our *Song*.

THE STEAMBOAT

GREENFIELD

CAPT. D. W. REED, will leave HARTFORD, from the foot of Talcott-st., to-morrow morning,

WEDNESDAY,

October 27th, at 7 1-2 o'clock, for the purpose of conveying Delegates to the MASS CONVENTION, to assemble at MIDDLETOWN, at 10 o'clock of the same day—returning in the afternoon.

Fare each way, 25 Cents. --- Children half price.

boats, began running between Newport and Providence, Rhode Island, in 1847. Masters of sailing vessels made fun of the smoky little steamer, and offered to carry their passengers free if they could not beat her. No one had much faith in steam. When President Monroe refused a ride up the Sound in the *Firefly*, her owner gave up the business.

Five years later, however, steamboats came to the Sound to stay. The *Fulton* and the *Connecticut*, bigger boats with gleaming copper boilers, began a regular summer service to Providence. They were followed by other boats, including the *Lexington*, which was built in 1835. She was 205 feet long and could make sixteen miles an hour.

In 1847 the steamer *Bay State* began regular runs to Fall River, Massachusetts, and that was the start of the old Fall River Line. The *Bay State* was 300 feet long and 40 feet wide, and was lit by oil lamps at night. Dinner was served at long candlelit tables and cost fifty cents.

Business was good, and more boats were added to the line. By 1869 it was owned by Jim Fisk, a well-known financier. Two of his boats were the *Bristol* and the *Providence*, each of which weighed nearly 3,000 tons and could carry more than 800 passengers. Fisk filled them with thick carpets and fine fixtures. He hired bands to serenade the customers, and in each boat he placed 250 canaries in cages.

Then came a whole fleet of floating palaces, including the *Commonwealth* and the *Priscilla*. Another famous boat was the *Pilgrim*. She slept 1,200 persons and was advertised as being lighted "with 1,000 in-

failed to take on enough coal. Just south of Yonkers, his boat ran out of fuel. Law was desperate. He ordered the crew to gather up all the loose chairs and benches and throw them on the fires. And, after the chairs and benches were gone, the crew ripped out wooden berths, doors, and even expensive paneling.

Black wood smoke poured from the *Oregon's* stacks. The crowds on shore roared as she sailed past and reached the Battery, only a few lengths ahead of the *C. Vanderbilt*. George Law had made good his boast, and the *Oregon* was the queen of the Sound and the river.

At the time of the great race, steamboats were still rather strange and wonderful to ordinary landlubbers. After all, it was only thirty years since steamboats had first sailed the tricky waters of Long Island Sound. The *Firefly*, one of the early candescent electric lights . . . Mr. Edison has exhausted his inventive faculties in fitting up this magnificent vessel."

Leaving New York, boats of the Fall River Line traveled up the Hudson River, through Hell Gate, then up the Sound, past Newport, to Fall River. Passengers making the return trip from Boston could take an afternoon train and be in Fall River in time for dinner aboard the boat. After a comfortable night's sleep, they would reach New York in the morning.

There were other steamboat lines on the Sound, but none were so famous as the old Fall River. Songs were written about it. Nearly all the Presidents and most of the famous people of the times traveled on it. And in ninety years, in spite of storms and accidents, the line lost only one passenger.

But faster trains, cheaper railroad fares, and automobiles put the Fall River line out of business. The last of its grand old steamers made their final run in 1937.

Commodore Vanderbilt's Lexington *was the floating palace of her day. When she caught fire, only four were saved out of about 140 aboard.*

Dr. Frank Wilson

by W.K. Hewitt   N. Currier, Lith & Pub. 2 Spruce St N Y

Awful Conflagration of the Steam boat **LEXINGTON** In Long Island Sound on Monday Eve? Jan? 13th 1840. by which melancholy occurrence; over 100 PERSONS PERISHED.

When the Old Streets Talked

In New York City around the middle of the 19th Century almost anything for the household could be bought on the crowded streets. Fruits, vegetables, meats, bread, oysters—all were sold outdoors by street vendors. There were also men who did special kinds of work, like cleaning boots or chimneys.

Some street vendors walked about on foot. Some had horses and wagons. Others had stands which they set up in the same spot every day. One old apple woman sat in a chair by the front door of A. T. Stewart's dry goods store for many years. When the store moved, the old woman stayed away until Mr. Stewart himself saw to it that her chair was moved and placed exactly as before.

Whether they walked, rode, sat or stood, all the street vendors cried their wares to attract business. They made the old streets ring with their talk.

Passers-by in old New York bought refreshing root beer at three cents a glass.

The Boots Cleaner.

"Strawberries! Fine, ripe, and red!"

"Here's beans, peas, cucumbers, cabbage, onions! Here they GO!"

George Cousin, the Patent Chimney Sweep
Cleaner, cried: "Sweep! Sweep! O!"

The Whale Oil Man.

The baker cart (right) carried bread through the streets. The charcoal man (below) had a curious sign.

The lemon and orange stand sold fruit "very fine, very cheap."

The oyster stand (right) sold oysters, well salted, for a cent or two apiece. The ice man (below) was described in a comic poem as carrying "a glorious lump of gleaming ice—'Ice! Rockland Ice!'"

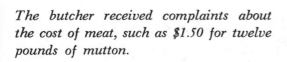

The butcher received complaints about the cost of meat, such as $1.50 for twelve pounds of mutton.

The volunteer firemen were proud of their daring rescues.

The Proud, Fighting Firemen

In the days before steam fire engines, the volunteer fireman was a proud fellow. He was proud of himself, and of his fire company. He was proud of his speed in racing through the streets, pulling carts that carried equipment. He was proud of his strength in working the hand pumps, which pumped water on the blaze. He was proud of his bravery in plunging into burning buildings to make daring rescues.

But he was not too proud to fight. In fact, he enjoyed it. And, most of all, he enjoyed fighting other firemen. This happened when two fire companies reached a fire at the same time. There was sure to be a glorious fight to decide which company would use the nearest hydrant. Or one company would send its toughs to stop another company from answering the same alarm, or prevent it from reaching the scene

This scene shows the new steam fire engines being used alongside the old-fashioned hand pumps of the volunteer fire companies.

of a fire. Putting out a fire was an honor each company wanted for itself.

Some of the fights lasted so long that the buildings burned down. But no one complained very much. After all, the volunteer firemen were heroes. At the first clang of the alarm bell they would drop their work or jump out of bed. They often risked their lives, and they were not paid a penny.

Even so, the fire companies had no trouble getting members. Merchants and clerks, artists and lawyers, butchers, bakers, bankers, bricklayers—all became smoke-eaters. Working side by side at a

Illustrations from the Historical Collection of the Insurance Company of North America

fire might be the mayor, the president of the bank, the leading lawyer. And with them might be the town toughs, ready and anxious for a fight.

It was so much fun and adventure to be a fireman that the volunteers refused to change their way of putting out fires. They would have nothing to do with the new-fangled steam fire engines, which had been used in England since 1832.

Then, in 1853, volunteers fought savagely in the streets of Cincinnati while a building burned to the ground. Cincinnati was through with volunteers. The city council ordered a steam engine and hired men to run it. When the new engine answered its first alarm, 250 angry volunteers turned up to give the city firemen a beating. But the fire chief had known what to expect. He had a small army of strong men with him, and they fought off the volunteers while the hired firemen did their job.

The steam fire engine was a big success in Cincinnati, and soon other cities were using them. At first they were drawn by men, but by 1870 most companies had horse-drawn engines. Firemen did less fighting, but they were still proud. They polished their engines until they shone. They bought matched teams of horses, training them well. The moment the alarm sounded, the firemen would go into action.

Today, modern fire trucks have replaced the old steam engines. All American cities have paid fire departments, but there are volunteer companies in some small towns. And, paid or not, firemen are still proud of their gleaming fire trucks, of their own daring and skill in putting out fires.

Flying horses and smoking steam engines were a thrilling sight as they raced to the scene of a fire.

The Great Bicycle Craze

In the 1890's, a new kind of bicycle went on sale in stores all over America. It was the safety bicycle, different from the old high-wheeler. Both front and back wheels were the same size, and the rubber tires were pumped full of air.

Anybody could ride a safety bicycle, and everybody seemed to want one. This was the beginning of the great bicycle craze of the Gay Nineties. It led to a change in the style of clothing and made people interested in better roads.

More than 500 factories were turning out bicycles, and a million of them were in use. Armories, roller skating rinks, and dance halls were changed into riding schools where beginners were taught how to handle a bike. In 1895 the New York *Tribune*, one of the city's biggest newspapers, said that the bicycle was of more importance to mankind than all the victories and defeats of Napoleon.

The craze reached its peak in 1896, and it was over by 1900. But while it lasted, songs were written about bicycles; special bicycle magazines were widely read; and the sports pages of newspapers gave more space to bicycle racing than they did to baseball.

It is not surprising that bicycles became popular. At the time, travel by horse was

slow, and travel by train was inconvenient. With a bicycle, people could ride out to the country or even visit another town. And if they were real "sports," they could go in for trick riding or racing.

People everywhere joined bicycle clubs and went on group trips to the countryside. In New York City, there was a club for men sixty or more years old. Other clubs liked to ride at night, carrying Japanese lanterns. Some clubs even had

People even sang about bicycles during the bicycle craze. This song sheet of 1895 has a message, too.

The pictures on this page are from a book called Bicycling for Ladies. *They show how to carry a bicycle, how to walk it, and how to ride. The last picture shows coasting—without coaster brakes.*

special yells. Members of the Lakeside Cycle Club, near Cleveland, used to shout: "Rah, rah; ziss, boom, bah! Who are we? Who are we? We are the people of the L.C.C.! Lakeside, Cleveland, O-hi-O!"

Doctors made statements in newspapers and magazines about the wonderful effects of cycling. They said that not in 200 years had there been anything of such great benefit to mankind.

To young people in their teens, bicycles were especially welcome. There was little for them to do in the small towns. There were no public swimming pools, few libraries. Keeping a riding horse was too expensive. Baseball and basketball had not yet swept the country.

Most of the young riders were interested in racing, and tried to look like professional racers. They turned their handles low, like a ram's horns, and leaned far forward when they rode. They stripped their bicycles of mudguards, chain guards, and anything else that added weight.

These sporting types rode as fast as they could, "scorching" the roads at speeds of ten or twelve miles an hour They frightened horses, and were chased by dogs. People on foot jumped out of their way and wondered what the world was coming to. Why, it was getting so a body risked his life every time he crossed the street!

Not many young children had bicycles. They were too expensive, costing from $100 to $125. The coming of the interurban electric railways and the first automobiles helped to end the great bicycle craze. Grownups gave their bicycles to the children, who had a fine time with them. They have been having a fine time riding bicycles ever since.

American Posters

Americans of the early 19th Century did not have many pictures to look at. There were no illustrated magazines, and, of course, no television or motion pictures. Even in cities there were few places where paintings were on display.

And so, when posters appeared in the early 1830's, they were welcomed by people starved for amusement. They were pasted up on fences, sheds, and barns, and everyone looked at them. Small boys and girls, their eyes wide with amazement,

The original of this poster is four feet high. Made in 1832, it is perhaps the oldest in America.

would stare at the posters again and again, and talk about the strange sights and scenes.

The first posters were used to advertise traveling wild animal shows, and were in black and white. Soon new methods of printing, such as lithography, were producing posters in bright colors. They were used to advertise all sorts of things, including stage plays and patent medicines.

Wind, rain, and time have destroyed most of the old posters, but enough of them still remain to show how wonderful they must have seemed to Americans of an earlier day.

Suspenders were only one of the many types of merchandise advertised on posters.

187

Theatrical posters helped attract crowds to all kinds of stage productions, from plays about the ever-popular Davy Crockett to minstrel shows. A minstrel show poster is shown on pages 190 and 191.

188

300 NIGHTS IN NEW YORK   THE GREAT SUCCESS

THE GIRL I LEFT BEHIND ME —

DIRECTION OF
GUSTAVE FROHMAN

BY BELASCO & FYLES

"SHE IS DEAD"

HAVERLY'S MINSTRELS AS THEY A
THE INAU

**RED BY SPECIAL INVITATION AT
ATION OF PRESIDENT GARFIELD·**

TO BE SEEN IN
J. M. FRENCH'S GREAT ORIENTAL CIRCUS!
AND EGYPTIAN CARAVAN!

COMING!
THE MASTODON
OF THE AGE!

192

W. W. COLE'S NEW 9 SHOWS CONSOLIDATED.

FOUR HANDSOME CELEBRITIES AND THEIR BAREBACK STEEDS WHO ARE MEMBERS OF THE LARGE TROUPE OF RIDERS.

CIRCUS, AMPHITHEATER, MENAGERIE, BICYCLE COLLEGE, RUSSIAN ROLLER SKATERS, GALLERY OF WAX STATUARY, MUSEUM, ENCYCLOPEDIA AND RACES.

WITH THE GREAT

W YORK AND NEW ORLEANS

ZOOLOGICAL AND EQUESTRIAN EXPOSITION!

ng on 60 Railroad Cars: 1000 Men. Horses and Animals!

VAN AMBURGH & CO$ MAMMOTH MENAGERIE.
THE ONLY LIVING GIRAFFE IN AMERICA.

H. FROST, General Director.   HENRY BARNUM, Manager.

Early posters for animal shows and circuses were more exciting than accurate, as shown by the hippo's mouthful of fierce tusks (above, left). The wood engravings of the human pyramid and the acrobats were used in circus advertising.

(Next page) Lillian Russell, a stage star, had a whole poster to herself in 1896. ▶

AN AMERICAN BEAUTY

Direction
CANARY &
LEDERER

LILLIAN RUSSELL

Adventure for a Nickel

His sentence was finished in a ringing shriek, for Calamity had drawn a revolver and shot him, even while his sarcastic words left his lips, and he fell to the ground, wounded through the breast.

" 'So much for your lyin', you miserable whelp!' the girl cried. . . .

"Now she dashed away through the narrow gulch, catching with delight long breaths of the perfume of flowers which met her nostrils at every onward leap of her horse, piercing the gloom of the night with her dark, lovely eyes, searchingly, lest she should be surprised; lighting a cigar at full motion. . . ."

Four desperadoes, attracted by the glow of her cigar, leaped at her from ambush, their Colts flashing. She rode them down amid "howls of pain and rage, and curses too vile to repeat here." And away she galloped, unharmed, whooping like a Comanche.

Her escape was not surprising, for this was no ordinary girl. She was Calamity Jane, and the heroine of a dime novel. It was nothing for her to fight off assorted villains, Indians, and savage beasts—all in the same book.

In dime novels and nickel weeklies, children and pretty girls were always rescued from a terrible fate just in the nick of time.

Dime novels like those about Calamity Jane were first brought out in 1860 by a publisher named Erastus Beadle. The books had paper covers, and the stories were full of wild adventure. The early tales were supposed to be true, and they were about such real people as Daniel

WORK AND WIN

An Interesting Weekly for Young America.

No. 283.   NEW YORK, MAY 6, 1904.   Price 5 Cents.

FRED FEARNOT'S NEWSBOY FRIEND;
OR, A HERO IN RAGS. *By* HAL STANDISH.

Fred was about to rescue the child. But he saw a newsboy in ragged clothes drop an armful of papers. He dashed to the baby carriage, snatched the infant up in his arms, and sprang toward the sidewalk.

Tip Top Weekly

"An ideal publication for the American Youth"

Issued weekly· By Subscription, $2.50 per year. Entered as Second Class Matter at the N. Y. Post Office by STREET & SMITH

No. 251.   **Price, Five Cents.**

FRANK MERRIWELL'S PARTY

or THE CRUISE OF THE PETREL

BY BURT L. STANDISH

CRACK! CRACK! TWO PISTOL SHOTS RANG OUT, AND ELSIE HEARD THE VOICE OF BART HODGE CRYING, "TAKE THAT, YOU PRIZE BEAUTY."

Boone, Pontiac, Mad Anthony Wayne, Custer, and Billy the Kid.

Dime novels were popular from the start, and sold at newsstands all over the country. They were especially popular with boys. In time, as more and more companies printed more and more books, the price was reduced to five cents. Dime novels became nickel weeklies, with new ones on sale every week like magazines.

There were other changes, too. The writers ran out of real people and began to make up heroes of their own. Among the most famous were Nick Carter, a brave detective; Frank Merriwell, a star athlete at Yale; and Fred Fearnot, who made money on the stock market. Another was Frank Reade, Jr., who invented an electric boomerang, a steam man, a submarine sea serpent, and a number of flying machines. All these heroes had adventures everywhere in the world, and specialized in daring rescues of pretty girls.

Although the heroes always got the better of the villains, the stories were full of gunfights and crime. Many people thought that they were bad for boys. They called dime novels and nickel weeklies cheap fiction and "devil-traps for the young." Fathers warned their children that they would be spanked if they were caught reading *Nick Carter* or *Fame and Fortune Weekly*. And so boys would buy the nickel books secretly, and sneak out behind the woodshed to read them.

In spite of all the fuss, millions of the paper-back books were sold until 1910. And, if it were not for movies, radio, television, and comics, boys would be reading them yet.

◀ *No matter where the hero went, there always seemed to be a girl who needed his help.*

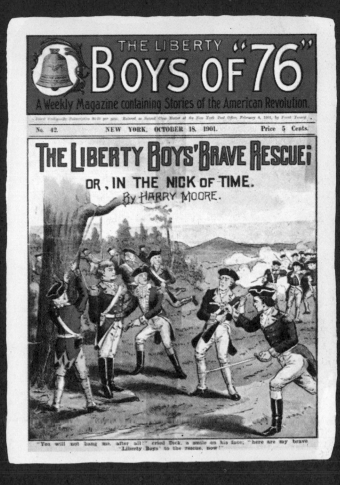

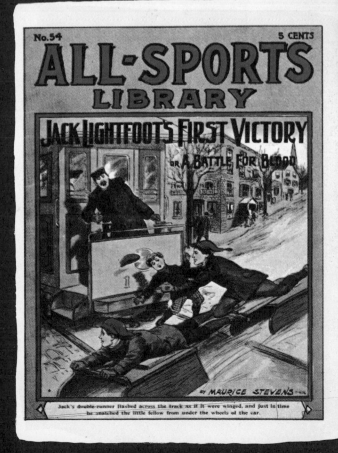

Courtesy Steelways published by the American Iron and Steel Institute

Building the Big Bridge

In the fall of 1873 a bearded man sat at the third-story back window of his home at 110 Columbia Heights, Brooklyn. Picking up a pair of field glasses, he looked out at the river. He was Washington Roebling, and he was watching the building of Brooklyn Bridge.

The bridge had been designed by his father, John Roebling, and work on it had started six years before. Then the older man died of tetanus from an accident that happened while surveying the bridge's route. Washington Roebling took up his father's work. He himself became sick from working in the compressed air of the

caissons—the big boxes which were sunk under water as the first step in making the bridge's towers.

Roebling was never really cured of his sickness, but he went on directing the work on the bridge. He taught his wife, Emily, engineering and mathematics so that she could carry instructions from him to his assistants.

For ten years he sat at the window, watching through his field glasses. He

A catwalk for the workmen on the big bridge was put up in 1877. It swayed in the wind and seemed dangerous, but no one ever fell from it. ▶

198

Just six days after the bridge was opened, a foolish rumor that it was falling caused a panic, and twelve persons were killed.

◄ Huge crowds turned out to see the opening of the big bridge linking Manhattan and Brooklyn, which had taken sixteen years to construct. A parade of steamers and sailing vessels of all kinds passed under it. In the evening, there was a display of fireworks. An artist of the time painted the scene as it looked to him.

Robert Odlum jumped off the new bridge as a stunt. He fell 140 feet to his death.

watched as a catwalk four feet wide was strung from the towers for use by the workmen. He watched the spinning of the cables. He watched the hanging of steel ropes from the cables to hold the floor beams. He saw girders, stays, trusses, and braces put in place. He saw the painting, the installation of electric lights and tracks for cable cars.

And he saw, one day, a cable break loose, whip through the air, and kill two men. It was the last of the accidents that happened during the building of the bridge, but it started talk. Some people shook their heads. Sooner or later, they said, the cables would break, and the bridge would come tumbling down.

Still, the work went on. And on May 24, 1883, sixteen years after it was started the bridge was opened, with bands and flags and fireworks, and the President of the United States among the crowd there to watch. Roebling watched too, from his window. About 100,000 people crossed it safely during the first twenty-four hours, and the big bridge stood.

The big bridge still stands today, spanning the waters between Brooklyn and the island of Manhattan, one of the engineering wonders of the world.

A rare photograph of chief mechanic Frank Farrington (extreme left) and his staff.

This fancily decorated locomotive was built around 1856.

Here Comes the Train!

From the beginning, there was adventure in American railroads. At first, there was the adventure of building locomotives that could run at all. After successful locomotives were built, there was the adventure of riding behind the puffing, snorting iron horse at speeds as high as thirty miles an hour.

In 1831, when the locomotive *De Witt Clinton* made its first run between Albany and Schenectady in New York state, stagecoach bodies were used for the cars. Some of the passengers sat on the top. Every time the train started or stopped, they would be jerked from their seats.

An advertisement showing the Hoosac Tunnel, a great engineering feat of its day.

201

The Amoskeag Manufacturing Company of Manchester, New Hampshire, was proud of this 4-4-0 locomotive. The first figure shows the number of wheels in the truck forward. The second figure shows the number of wheels in the main drive, while the last figure shows the number of wheels under the cab. This three-figure code was a quick and easy way to identify the various types of steam locomotives. It was widely used by railroad men and locomotive builders.

Anyone who had an umbrella put it up, as a protection from the smoke, sparks, coals, and cinders that poured from the smokestack. The umbrellas were of little help, for they soon caught fire.

People came from miles to see the train. A passenger on the first trip wrote: "Everybody . . . came from a distance with all kinds of conveyances. They drove as

The Old Print Shop

near as they could get, only looking for the best position to get a view of the train. As it approached, the horses took fright and wheeled, upsetting buggies, carriages and wagons . . . and it is not now positively known if some of them have yet stopped."

But soon the horses learned how to behave, and closed cars replaced the stagecoaches. Then came the adventure of lay-ing track from town to town, and, at last, in 1869, the rails stretched across mountain and prairie to the Pacific Coast. The chug-chug of locomotives stitched together the long miles of the continent, and the sweet, sad call of train whistles echoed from the lonely hills.

The coming of the railroad made some towns, like Chicago, Kansas City, and Los

The locomotive Arkansas, *shown in Indian country.*

Angeles, into cities. Other towns, too far from the rail lines, never grew. The railroads themselves became important business, and important businessmen schemed and fought for their control.

Rolling on the iron wheels went cattle from cow towns in the West, goods from factories of the East, emigrants bound for newly opened lands, and country boys seeking their fortune in the big city. And it was steam that made the wheels go around—steam in the hissing, roaring, rumbling locomotives. No wonder, then, that locomotive makers decorated the old coal burners with fancy lamps and iron work and enameled paintings.

But as always, men were looking for new ways of doing things. Around 1924 the first Diesel engine was used in the United States. Today, steam locomotives are vanishing rapidly and can be found mainly on the smaller railroads or on little sand and logging lines. Diesels and electric engines drive most of the trains.

In the 1860's and 70's herds of buffalo sometimes stopped the trains.

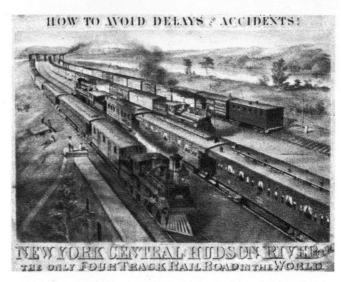

During the 1800's, railroads put out advertisements like these to attract passengers. Each line was proud of its special features. The New York Central and Hudson River Railroad boasted that it was "the only four track railroad in the world."

"The only American R.R. route to the West and Southwest," claimed the Lake Shore Railroad, which addressed its advertisement to the businessman, the pleasure traveler, and the emigrant in search of a home in the West.

The Erie Railway described itself as a "great trunk line and United States mail route between New York City and the Western States and Territories." Other lines featured safety, comfort, convenience, speed, low fares, beautiful scenery, and sleeping cars.

In the America of yesterday, an America of small towns and farms, the railroad station was an important place. It was a link with the outside world, and anyone who
did not have something better to do—and many who did—came down to the station

to watch the trains pull in. This picture, painted in 1867 by Edward Lampson Henry, is called The 9:45 Accommodation, Stratford, Connecticut. *"Accommodation" was the name given to a local train that connected elsewhere with the express.*

The Birdmen at Belmont

At Belmont most Americans, and a few Englishmen, flew biplanes. The one above is a Farman.

Airplanes flying backward! It wasn't possible. Yet thousands in the stands at Belmont Park, New York, saw it happen. It was October, 1910, at the most important international air meet ever held in America. The two slow planes in the air had suddenly hit a strong headwind that was faster than they were, making it appear to those on the ground that they were flying backward.

Fliers were in the headlines almost every day that month. October had started

Claude Grahame-White, a dashing English flier, surprised people in Washington by landing his plane on an avenue in front of the White House.

with an air race from Chicago to New York, in which the leading plane had given up thirty-two miles out of Chicago. Then in Atlantic City, Walter Wellman took off in a dirigible to cross the Atlantic. He went 400 miles, and was picked up by a steamer. And in St. Louis, ten balloons started a distance contest. The winner was picked up in the wilds of Canada after a record flight of 1,355 miles.

Thousands came to watch the big international air meet at Belmont. There were contests every day for more than a week. Sometimes as many as fourteen planes were in the air at the same time.

One of the big events was the Gordon Bennett 100-kilometer speed race. A Frenchman, Alfred LeBlanc, roared around the course and drew well ahead of the others. On his last lap he ran out of gas and crashed, but he was not badly hurt. Claude Grahame-White, an English flier, won the race. Then there was another race to the Statue of Liberty and back, for a $10,000 prize. John B. Moisant, an American, won the prize money.

No great records were set by the birdmen at Belmont. But by the time the meet was over, no one could doubt that the airplane was here to stay.

(Right) Sights like this thrilled the crowds at the Belmont Park race track. The picture shows (top to bottom) a Wright plane, a Farman, a Blériot, an Antoinette, and another Farman. ▶

A Liner, a U-Boat, and History

The liner was the Cunard steamship *Lusitania*. The U-boat was the German submarine *U-20*. And when the *Lusitania* left New York on May 1, 1915, bound for England, no one knew that the two vessels would make history.

The great ship carried 1,250 passengers, 188 of them American citizens. The United States was then at peace with the world, although in Europe World War I was already many months old. Some of the passengers aboard the *Lusitania* must have read the official German warning in the morning newspapers. It stated that Germany and Great Britain were at war, that the war zone included the British Isles, and that Americans who went to England on British ships did so at their own risk.

But the American travelers were not

The artist who made this drawing of the Lusitania *going down did not know that she sank stern end first.*

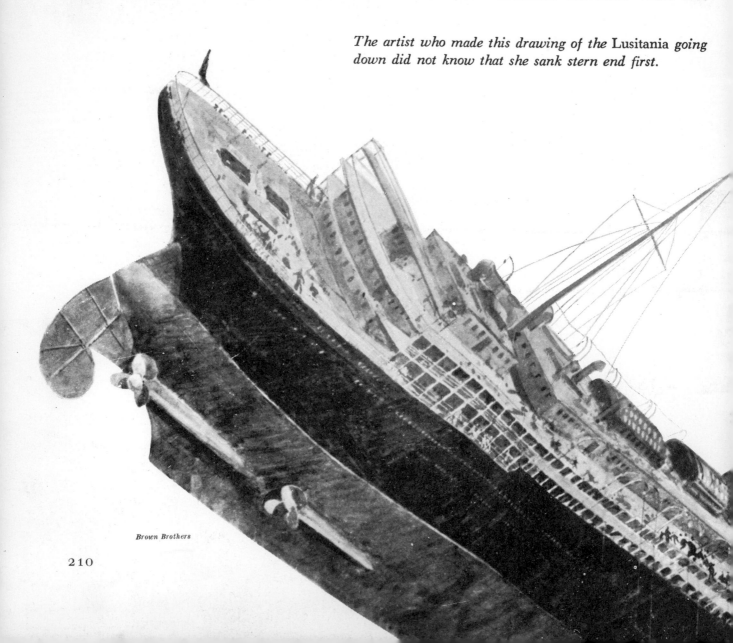

worried. The war seemed unreal and far away. Great Britain was one of the strongest sea powers on earth and would surely not risk her finest and largest passenger vessel. As for U-boats, they were slow and clumsy. Besides, there were not very many of them.

All went well for the liner as she crossed the Atlantic. On May 7th the passengers could see the coast of Ireland in the distance. Suddenly, without warning, the *Lusitania* was struck by a torpedo from a U-boat. A second explosion followed, and the ship sank quickly. Down to their death went 1,154 persons, including 114 Americans.

People in the United States were shocked, and feeling rose against Germany. President Woodrow Wilson warned that the United States would fight for freedom of the seas. Germany backed down for a time. But in 1917 her U-boats were out again, and the United States declared war.

This is the official German advertisement that appeared in New York newspapers on May 1, 1915, the day the British liner Lusitania *sailed from New York for England. Some of the American passengers on the ship probably saw the warning, but they paid no attention to it.*

News That's
to Print."

The New York Times.

EXTRA
5:30 A. M.

NEW YORK, SATURDAY, MAY 8, 1915.—TWENTY-FOUR PAGES.

ONE CENT

...ANIA SUNK BY A SUBMARINE, PROBABLY 1,260 DEAD; ...CE TORPEDOED OFF IRISH COAST; SINKS IN 15 MINUTES; ...PT. TURNER SAVED, FROHMAN AND VANDERBILT MISSING; ...WASHINGTON BELIEVES THAT A GRAVE CRISIS IS AT HAND

SOME DEAD TAKEN ASHORE

Several Hundred Survivors at Queenstown and Kinsale.

STEWARD TELLS OF DISASTER

One Torpedo Crashes Into the Doomed Liner's Bow, Another Into the Engine Room.

SHIP LISTS OVER TO PORT

Makes It Impossible to Lower Many Boats, So Hundreds Must Have Gone Down.

ATTACKED IN BROAD DAY

Passengers at Luncheon—Warning Had Been Given by Germans Be-

The head of the Lincoln statue as it looked with the wrong kind of lighting.

Light for Lincoln's Statue

Daniel Chester French, the sculptor, walked slowly up the steps of the Lincoln Memorial building in Washington. For eight years he had worked on the model for his statue of Abraham Lincoln. Now the statue itself, in marble, had just been placed in the building, and he had come to give it a few finishing touches.

At the entrance between the high columns, he stopped and stared at the statue before him. This was nothing he had made. The face of Lincoln looked strange, flat, frightened and startled.

French moved a little closer to the statue, and then he realized what had happened. This was his statue, all right. But the light was terribly wrong. It threw shadows in unexpected places, changing the expression of Lincoln's face.

Looking around, French saw that some daylight came in through the translucent marble ceiling. But a terrific glare came from the polished marble floor, and from the gleaming reflecting pool in front of the building. And this glare, which gave the statue more light from below than from above, was the cause of the trouble.

There was not time to do anything

The statue after sculptor French and engineers worked years to improve the lighting system.

about it, for the building was to be thrown open to the public on Memorial Day, May 30, 1922. French waited until the opening ceremonies were over, and then went to work with Henry Bacon, the architect who had designed the building. After dozens of experiments, they saw that they must use artificial lighting, and they asked the help of the General Electric Company.

Engineers began working with the model of the statue in French's studio in New York. They found a way to light it, but the method was complicated and expensive. French and Bacon would have to ask Congress for more money. Just as the two men were preparing their appeal to Congress, Bacon died.

For a time nothing was done, but Congress eventually voted to spend the money. Three more years went by before the engineers' plan was carried out. But at last the lighting system was set up, and the statue looked as it was meant to look.

Millions of people have since visited the Memorial. Standing before the statue, in the hush that fills the great hall, they can feel the majesty and the power of the man who was Abraham Lincoln.

213

INDEX

All page numbers in italics refer to captions.

Collection of the Insurance Company of North America

Adventure Galley (ship), 39
Airplanes, 208–210
Alexandria, Virginia, 122, 126, 131
Algonkians, 18
America, discovery of, 8–11
American Indians, *see* Indians
American Revolution, *see* Revolutionary War
Antietam, 133
Antilia, *8*, 11
Anti-Masons, 146
Apaches, 14, 86
Appomattox, *140*
Arapaho Indians, 16
Arkansas (locomotive), *204*
Arkansas Indians, 28
Arkansas River, 28
Ashley, W. H., 98
Assiniboins, *90*
Astor, John Jacob, 171
Atotarho, 19, 21

Bacon, Henry, 213
Bainbridge, William, 63
Baker, Jim, 98
Balling, Ole Peter Hansen, *133*
Baltimore, Maryland, 72, 113, 120, 121
Bartolozzi, Francesco, 109
Bay State (steamer), 176
Beadle, Erastus, 195
Beauregard, Pierre G. T., 135
Bellamy, Samuel, 35
Belmont Park, New York, 208–209
Bicycles, 185–186

Bierstadt, Albert, *88*
Billy the Kid, 197
Blackbeard, *34*, 39
Blackfoot Indians, 16, *90*, 98
Blair, Francis P., Jr., 132–133
Bodmer, Karl (Charles), *15*, *89*, *90*
Bonneville, Benjamin, 96
Bonny, Anne, *39*
Boone, Daniel, 49, 195, 197
Borgne, Lake, 72
Boston, Massachusetts, 83, 113, 129, 177
Brady, Mathew, *166*
Brewster & Company, 169–172
Bridger, Jim, 100
Bristol (steamboat), *173*, 176
Brooklyn Bridge, 198–200
Bryan, William Jennings, *145*
Buffaloes, *85*, *87*, *88*, 96–97, 118, *204*
Bull Run, battles of, 133, 135
Burnside, Ambrose E., 133
Butterfield, John, 152
Bygrave, William, *113*

C. Vanderbilt (steamboat), 173–176
Cadmus (ship), 79
California, 103, 113, 152
Campaigns, political, 144–151
Canada, 25, 26, 27, 32, 70, 71, 130
Cape Hatteras, 139
Carolina (war schooner), 73
Carriages, horse, 169–172
Carson, Kit, 100, 101, 102, 103
Carter, Nick, 197
Catlin, George, 87
Cayugas, 18, 21
Champlain, Lake, *70*, 71
Chancellorsville, battle of, 135
Chesapeake (ship), *65–67*, 68
Cheyenne Indians, 16, 102
Chicago, Illinois, 129, 130, *151*, 203, 208
Chinaware, 76–77
Chippewas, 15
Cincinnati, Ohio, 183
Civil War, 51, 53, *109*, 122–141, *148*
Clay, Henry, 146
Clermont (steamboat), 79
Cleveland, Grover, *148*, *151*
Clipper ships, 112–117

Columbus, Christopher, 8–11
Comanches, 16
Commonwealth (steamer), 176
Concord, battle of, 127
Congress (frigate), 138
Connecticut (steamboat), 176
Constellation (frigate), 120–121
Constitution (frigate), 63, *64–65*, 68
Constitution, U. S., 145
Conventions, political, 144–151
Cook, John, 170
Copley, John, 58
Cornelius, Robert, 165
Coroas, 28
Cotton gin, invention of the, 51–52
Country stores, 156–160
Crees, *90*
Crevecoeur (fort), 27
Crook, George, *132–133*
Crow Indians, 16
Cumberland (frigate), 138
Custer, George A., *132–133*, 154–155, 197
Cutty Sark (clipper ship), 113

Daguerreotypes, *161–163*, *165*
Dakota Indians, 15
Davis, Jefferson (Confederate President), 140–141
Davis, Jefferson (General), *132–133*
Decatur, Stephen, 63, 68, 79
Deganawidah, 18–19, 21
Delaware River, 54–57
Derby, Elias Hasket, 83
Devin, Thomas, *132–133*
De Witt Clinton (locomotive), 201
Dime novels, 195
Drake, Sir Francis, 35
Dude ranch, first, 118–119

Eastman, Seth, *91*
Ellis, Colonel, *163*
Ellsworth, Elmer Ephraim, *122*, 123, 126, 129–131
Emory, W. H., *132–133*
Endymion (ship), 68
Erickson, John, *139*
Erie, Lake, 26, 27
  battle of, *62*, 63, 70–71
Ewell, Richard S., 134

Fall River, Massachusetts, *174*, 176, 177
Fall River Line, 173–177
Farny, Henry F., 95
Farrington, Frank, *200*
Ferris, J. L. G., *44*
Filson, John, 49
Firefly (steamboat), 176
Firemen, 130, *164–165*, 182–184
Fisk, Jim, 176
Fitzpatrick, Thomas, 100
Flying Cloud (clipper ship), 113
Flying Fish (clipper ship), 113
Forts, *see* names of forts
Fox, Gustavus V., 138, 139
Franklin, Benjamin, 45, 61, 79
Fredericksburg, 133
Frémont, John Charles, 101, 102–105
Frémont Lake, 118
Frémont Peak, 103–105
French, Daniel Chester, 212–213
Frontenac, Count, 25
Frontenac, Fort, 25
Fulton (steamboat), 176
Fulton, Robert, *58*, 79

Gardiners Island, 39
General Electric Company, 213
George III, King, 58
Gettysburg, 133, 141
Glass, Hugh, 100
Godey, Alexis, *102*
Gordon, John Brown, 134
Grahame-White, Claude, 208
Grant, Ulysses S., 133, *140*, *144*
Great Lakes, *see* names of lakes
Green Bay, 27
Greene, Mrs. Nathaniel, 51
Greene, S. Dana, 137–139
Griffin (ship), 26, 27
Gros Ventres Indians, 102
Guerrière (ship), 63
Guns, Whitney's, 52–53

Hamilton, Alexander, *58*
Hampton, Virginia, 39
Hampton, Wade, 134
Hampton Roads, Virginia, 136, 138
Hancock, Winfield S., *132–133*
Harrison, Benjamin, 150, *151*
Harrison, William Henry, 71, 146, 150
Heartbreak, Fort, 27
Henry, Edward Lampson, 207
Hesselius, John, 58
Hessians, 54, 56, 57
Hiawatha, 18, 21
Hill, Ambrose P., 134, 135
Hobart, Garret A., *147*

Hoffbauer, Charles, 134
Honeyman, John, 54–57
Hood, John Bell, 134
Hooker, Joseph, 133
Hoosac Tunnel, *201*
Howard, Oliver O., *132–133*
Howland, Esther, *108*
Hudson River, 173, 175, 177
Hull, Isaac, 63
Huron, Lake, 27
Hurons, 18

Illinois River, 27
Indians, American, *see also* names of tribes, 12–23, 27, 41, 44, 85–100, 102–103, 146, 153, 154–155, 163, *204*
Ino (clipper ship), 113
Insurgente (ship), 121
Iowa Indians, 16
Iroquois, 12, 18, 21

Jackson, Andrew, 72–75, 146
Jackson, Thomas J. "Stonewall," 134, 135
Jamestown, Virginia, 40
Java (frigate), *64–65*
Jefferson, Thomas, 59, 61, 146
Johnston, Joseph E., 135
Jones, Jacob, 63
Jones, John Paul, *59*

Kidd, Captain William, 39
Kilpatrick, Judson, *132–133*
Klir, Joseph, *151*

La Cosa, Juan de, 8, 10
Lafayette, 79
Laramie, Fort, 102
La Salle, Robert Cavelier, Sieur de, 24–33
Law, George, 173, 175, 176
Lawrence (brig), 71
Lawrence, James, *62*, 63, *65*
League of Five Nations, 18
LeBlanc, Alfred, 208
Lee, Fitzhugh, 134
Lee, Robert E., 133, 134, 135, 140–141
Lewis and Clark expedition, 61, 98
Lexington (steamboat), 176, *177*
Lexington, battle of, 127
Lightning (clipper ship), *112–113*
Lincoln, Abraham, 123, 130, 133, *148*, 150, 212–213
Lincoln Memorial (Washington), 212–213

Little Big Horn, Battle of the, 154–155
Locomotives, 201–205
Logan, John A., *132–133*
Long Island Sound, 173, 176, 177
Longstreet, James, 134
Lorillard, Pierre, *171*
Los Angeles, California, 152, 203–205
Louis XIV, King, 29
Louis XV, King, 45
Louisbourg, 45–48
Louisiana, 29, 146
Lusitania (steamship), 210–211

Macdonough, Thomas, 63, *70*, 71
Macedonian (ship), 68
Mandan Indians, *19*, *22–23*
Mason, J. C., 142
Masons, 146
Mato-topa, *23*
Maximilian, Prince, *90*
McClellan, George B., 133, *148*
McDowell, Irvin, 133
McKinley, William, *146–147*, 150
McPherson, James B., *132–133*
Meade, George G., 133
Memphis, Tennessee, 142, 143
Merrimac (warship), 136–139
Merriwell, Frank, 197
Merritt, Wesley, *132–133*
Mexico, war with, 128
Michigan, Lake, 27
Milling machine, Whitney's, 52
Minnesota (frigate), *136*, 138
Mississippi River, 24–33, 73, 75, 142–143
Missouri River, 28, *90*, 98
Mobile, Alabama, 72
Mohawk Indians, 18, 21
Moisant, John B., 208
Monitor (warship), 136–139
Monroe, Fort, 138
Monroe, James, 176
Morgan, J. Pierpont, 172
Morse, Samuel F. B., 162
Mount Vernon, New York, 59
Mountain men, 98–101
Mower, Joseph A., *132–133*
Musketeers, 40–41

Naiche (Indian chief), 86
Natchez, 14, 28
Navahos, 14
New Jersey, 54–57
New Orleans, battle of, 72–75
New York City, New York, 38, 39, 68, 93, 113, 121, 130, 137,

152, 169, 170, 173, 174–175, 177, 178, 185, 198–200, 208, 210, 213
Niagara (ship), *70*, 71
Niagara Falls, 25, *161*
Niagara River, 25, *26–27*
Nickel weeklies, 195–197
Niña, 8
Norfolk, Virginia, 58, 121, 139
Norsemen, 10
North Carolina, *12–13*, 39
Northampton, Massachusetts, 169

Odlum, Robert, *199*
"Old Ironsides," *see Constitution*
Oneidas, 18, 21
Onondagas, 18, 19, 21
Ontario, Lake, 25, 26
Ord, E. O. C., *132–133*
Oregon (steamboat), 173–176
Oregon Trail, 103
Overland Stage, 152–153

Pakenham, General, *73*, 75
Palmer, Francis, 95
Parke, John G., *132–133*
Patriot (bark), *83*
Peabody, Joseph, 83
Peale, Charles Wilson, 58–61
Peale, Raphaelle, 59
Peale, Rembrandt, *58*, 59, *60*
Pehriska-Ruhpa, *15*
Pepperell, Sir William, 45
Perry, Oliver Hazard, *62*, 63, 70–71
Philadelphia, Pennsylvania, 55, 59, 61, 87, *161*
Photography, early, 161–168
Pickett, George Edward, 141
Piegans, 16
Pilgrim (steamer), 176
Piombo, Sebastiano del, *11*
Pirates, 34–39, 121
Political conventions, 144–151
Pope, John, 133
Porcelain, 79
Porter, David, 63
Posters, early American, 187–194
Pottery, English, 78–79
President (frigate), 63, 68
Princeton, New Jersey, 59, *60*
Priscilla (flagship), 174–175, 176
Privateering, 35, 81, 83
Providence (steamer), 176
Providence, Rhode Island, 176

Railroads, 153, 201–207
Rall, Colonel, 56–57
Rawlins, John A., *132–133*

Read, Mary, *39*
Remington, Frederick, *92*, 93, *152*
Reno, Major, 154
Revere, Paul, 63
Revolutionary War, 54–57, 59, 61, 81, 127, 128
Roberts, Bartholomew, *38*
Rockefeller, John D., *169*
Rockefeller, William, 172
Roebling, John, 198
Roebling, Washington, 198, 200
Rogers' Rangers, *44*
Rogers' Rock, battle of, *44*
Roosevelt, Franklin D., 150
Roosevelt, J. R., 172
Roosevelt, Theodore, *149*
Russell, Charles M., 95

St. Joseph River, 27
St. Louis, Missouri, 99, 102, 208
Salem, Massachusetts, 80–84
Salt Lake City, Utah, 153
San Francisco, California, 113, 152, *162–163*, 166–167
Santa Maria, 8
Santo Domingo, *35–37*
Schenectady, New York, 201
Schofield, John M., *132–133*
Schreyvogel, Charles, 91
Seneca Indians, 18, 21, *23*, 25
Seven Days' Battle, 133
Sewell's Point, 138
Seymour, Horatio, *144*
Shannon (frigate), *65–67*, 68
Sheridan, Philip, 133
Sherman, William T., 133
Silsbee, Nathaniel, 82
Sioux Indians, 15, *91*, 102, 154
Slaves, 52, 53, 61
Slocum, Henry W., *132–133*
Smith, Jed, 100, 101
Smuggling, 38
Snake Indians, *16*
South Pass, 102, 103, 153
Sovereign of the Seas (clipper ship), 113
Stagecoaches, 152–153
Stewart, A. T., 178
Stewart, Sir William Drummond, 118–119
Street vendors, 178–181
Stuart, James E. B. "Jeb," 135
Sultana (steamboat), 142–143
Sweetwater Trail, 103

Taensas, 28
Tammany Hall, *144*
Taos, 101
Taylor, Zachary, 146
Terry, Alfred H., *132–133*

Thomas, George H., *132–133*
Tipton, Missouri, 152
Tories, 54, 56
Trains, 201–207
Trenton, New Jersey, 54, 57, 59, *60*
Tuscaroras, 18
Tyler, John, *149*, 150

U-20 (submarine), 210–211
Ulysses (ship), *84*
Underhill, Captain, 41
Union Pacific Railroad, 153
United States (frigate), 63, 68

Valentines, 106–111
Van Buren, Martin, 150
Vanderbilt, Cornelius, *170*, 173, 175, 177
Vaughan, William, 48
Vengeance (warship), 121
Vespucci, Amerigo, 10
Virginia, 39, 133, 141
Volunteer militia companies, 127–131, *163*

Waldseemüller, Martin, 10, *11*
War of 1812, 62–75, 83, 121
Warren, G. K., *132–133*
Washington, D. C., 72, 122, *208*
Washington, George, 54–57, 58, 59, *60*, 61, *77*, 79
Washington, Martha, *77*
Wayne, Mad Anthony, 197
Webb, Dr. W. S., *169*
Wellman, Walter, 208
Wells, Fargo, 153
West, Benjamin, 58
West Indies, 32, 38, 81
Whigs, *145*, *149*
White Bull, Chief, 154–155
Whitney, Eli, 50–53
Wilkes-Barre, Pennsylvania, 87
Williams, Old Bill, 98, 101
Wilson, Woodrow, 211
Wind River Mountains, *99*, 118
Wirt, William, 146
Witch of the Waves (clipper ship), 113
Wolfe, General, 55
Worcester, Massachusetts, *108*, *167*
Worden, Captain, 138

Yankees, Louisbourg taken by, 45–48
Yankton Indians, *90*

Zephyr (clipper ship), 113, *114–115*
Zouaves, 122, 129–131